Southern Light

Stories That Guide Us Home

Charles E. Cravey

In His Steps Publishing

ISBN: 978-1-58535-091-9 (Soft)

ISBN: 978-1-58535-092-6 (Hard)

ISBN: 978-1-58535-093-3 (Kindle)

Library of Congress Catalog Number: 2025910422

Published by In His Steps Publishing, Statesboro, Georgia

DISCLAIMER: All characters in this book are fictional.

Contents

Introduction

Light speaks differently in the South. It whispers through Spanish moss at dawn, dances across dark swamp waters at dusk, and transforms ordinary moments into sacred memories. Here, where history hangs as heavy as August humidity, light doesn't just illuminate—it reveals, transforms, and sanctifies.

This collection of essays explores the sacred geography of Southern light, from the highest peak of Brasstown Bald to the darkest depths of the Okefenokee. Each story captures a particular quality of illumination unique to our region: the way morning light filters through cathedral live oaks in Savannah, how sunset sets Louisiana's cane fields ablaze, or how phosphorescent waves paint Jekyll Island's shore with living light.

These are not just observations of natural phenomena, but meditations on how light shapes our understanding of place, memory, and spirit. Through these pages, we witness how the South's particular quality of light has influenced our art, architecture, and soul—how it has shaped not just what we see, but who we are.

From the lamplighters of Charleston to the light-chasers of River Street, from the swamp lights of the Okefenokee to the star-filled skies above Angel Oak, these stories remind us that in the South, light itself becomes story, becomes history, becomes prayer.

Charles E. Cravey, May 2025

Dedicated to

The Giver of Light and Life – Jesus Christ!

To God be the Glory!

Amen.

1

Evening Walk, Memory's Grace

Some loves can't be measured in miles or minutes, but in footsteps shared and sunsets witnessed. For thirty years, they walked that weathered pier at St. Simons together, their evening ritual as faithful as the tide. Every night, just as the sun began its descent, they'd make their way past the fishing folks with their buckets and hopes, past the young lovers learning what these two had known for decades, all the way to the pier's end where sky meets sea.

She'd wear that blue sweater, no matter the season—"Evening air has teeth," she'd say—and he'd carry those old binoculars, more habit than necessity. They never needed magnification to see what mattered. Their bench, smooth from years of faithful sitting, waited like an old friend. Some evenings they'd talk, their voices low and comfortable as worn leather. Other times they'd just sit, letting the symphony of wind and wave speak for them.

He knew every board of that pier, every creak and groan, the specific way salt air wrapped around them like a blessing. She knew how to read his silence, the way his eyes would follow the shrimp boats home, how his hand would find hers just as the sun touched the horizon—as if every sunset was their first and their last, all at once.

The ritual never varied: they'd arrive as the light turned golden, find their spot third bench from the end, and settle in like royalty taking their throne. She'd smooth her skirt, he'd wipe the bench with his handkerchief—though it was already clean—and together they'd watch God paint the sky. Sometimes dolphins would surface nearby, their fins cutting dark signatures across the golden water. Pelicans would dive like arrows into the surf, and sandpipers would dance their eternal ballet with the waves below.

Now, from his chair by the window overlooking a garden he no longer tends, he watches different sunsets. But in his heart, he's still walking that pier, her hand warm in his, their footsteps matched to the rhythm of waves below. The salt air still kisses his memory, and in his mind's eye, that golden light still catches in her silver hair just so.

Some folks might say it's sad that he can't make that walk anymore. But he knows better. Every evening, as the light grows soft, he closes his eyes and finds himself there—their bench, their sunset, their moment outside of time. Because love, like memory, knows no distance. And some walks never really end; they just continue in the heart.

In the deepening dusk of his room, if you listen carefully, you might hear him whisper, "Evening air has teeth." And somewhere, on a weathered pier reaching into the Georgia sea, two souls still walk hand in hand into the setting sun, their love as constant as the tide, as eternal as the evening star.

Some blessings, once given, belong to us forever. Some sunsets never truly end. They just move from our eyes to our hearts, where they keep on glowing, lighting our way home.

2

Evening Song at St. Simons

The sun doesn't just set over St. Simons Sound—it surrenders to the sea in a ceremony old as time itself. Tonight, like every night, the great gold disc melts into the horizon while shrimp boats drift home on the tide, their outriggers sketching calligraphy against the painted sky. The light catches in the rigging, turning ordinary rope and steel into strings of diamonds.

Old salts like Captain Marcus Tidewater know this is more than just another day's end. Standing at the wheel of the "Miss Jenny," named for his grandmother who taught him to read the waters, he watches the sun's descent with the reverence of a man who's witnessed this miracle ten thousand times and still finds it holy.

"Most folks think the sunset's about the sun," he says, weathered hands resting easy on the helm. "But it's really about everything the light touches before it goes—how it turns the marsh grass to spun gold, how it makes the whole sound look like heaven's own harbor, how it reminds us that endings are just beginnings turned around backward."

The evening light writes secrets on the water in a language only pelicans seem to read. They dive through the gilt-edged waves like exclamation points punctuating God's own poetry. Behind them, Jekyll Island's ancient oaks hold the last light in their Spanish moss like grandmothers cradling precious things.

This is the hour when time itself seems to slow, when the boundary between earth and heaven grows thin as smoke. Somewhere beyond the lighthouse, tomorrow is already happening, but here in this moment, eternity touches time with golden fingers. The marsh grass whispers prayers older than Christianity, and even the fiddler crabs seem to pause in their endless scuttling to watch the sky's transformation.

As purple shadows claim the waterway and the first stars begin their shy emergence, Captain Marcus turns his bow toward home. The channel markers blink their red and green guidance, but he hardly needs them—sixty years of sunsets have taught him to read these waters by heart. He knows that even in darkness, the way home is lit by memory, by instinct, by the kind of wisdom that lives in the bones.

"People come from all over to watch our sunsets," he reflects, as the running lights paint soft circles on the darkening water. "They bring their cameras, their phones, trying to capture it. But the real beauty isn't in what you can photograph—it's in how it makes you feel, like you're part of something bigger than yourself, something that was here long before you and will be here long after. That's what these waters teach us, if we're quiet enough to learn."

Behind him, St. Simons Light begins its nightly vigil, its beam a finger of grace touching island and sea, marking the thin line between what was and what will be. Tomorrow, the sun will rise again over the marsh, pelicans will dive through gilt-edged waves, and Captain Marcus will guide the "Miss Jenny" out into the sound. But for now, in this moment between day and dream, the world holds its breath, and even time itself seems to pause in reverence.

This is how evening comes to the Golden Isles—not with fanfare, but with grace, writing its ancient promise across the sky: Beauty endures. Love remains. Tomorrow comes.

3

Dawn's First Light

Blue Ridge Benediction

High above Clayton, where Highway 76 weaves through the ancient shoulders of the Blue Ridge, dawn doesn't so much arrive as it unfolds—a slow revelation of grace. First comes the choir of whip-poor-wills, their songs trailing off like ellipses into the darkness. Then the eastern sky begins its gradual transformation, painting itself in colors that defy naming—not quite purple, not quite rose, something between promise and fulfillment.

Herb McClure, who's lived all his eighty-three years on this mountain, stands on his porch with a tin cup of coffee growing cold in his hands. He's watched this same miracle for most of those years, but like true love and good bourbon, some things never grow ordinary with repetition.

"Mountain morning," he says softly, as if naming a prayer, "is God's way of showing off." The mist rises from the valleys like incense, holy smoke ascending from nature's own altar. Through gaps in the fog, you can see the

quilted patterns of small farms and woodlots, each one a
square in the great tapestry of mountain life.

The first light touches the highest ridges, setting the autumn sourwoods aflame. It slides down the mountainsides
like honey dripping slow, gathering in pools of gold in the
valleys, turning ordinary pastures into stained glass. Even
the cattle, dark shapes emerging from the morning mist,
seem to pause their grazing to witness this daily resurrection of light.

"People ask me why I never moved away," Herb reflects,
his voice carrying the melody of these hills in its cadence.
"But how do you leave a place where every morning reminds you that beauty isn't just something you see—it's
something you belong to?"

As the sun finally crests the ridge, it sends shafts of light
through the morning mist like divine fingers touching the
earth. Everything they touch is transformed—dewdrops
become diamonds, spider webs turn to silver nets, and the
whole world seems new-made and full of possibility.

This is more than just another day beginning. This is
testimony, renewal, benediction. This is the mountains
reminding us that some things remain sacred, no matter
how the world changes in the valleys below.

4

Firefly Summer

On Grandma Lilly's wraparound porch in Screven County, summer evenings aren't measured by clocks but by fireflies. As day surrenders to dusk, the first tiny lights appear over her hydrangea bushes like stars deciding to dance closer to earth. That's when the counting begins—a tradition as sweet as the tea in mason jars sweating on the porch rail.

"Lightning bugs," Grandma Lilly always corrects anyone who calls them fireflies. "They're God's way of letting us know magic still lives in ordinary places." At eighty-nine, she's counted these evening lights through more summers than anyone else in the family, her front porch becoming a observatory of wonder for four generations.

Every evening from late May through early September, they gather—children, grandchildren, great-grandchildren—in the old wooden rockers and porch swing. The rules, established decades ago, remain simple: no phones, no counting out loud until the end, and everyone must stay still enough to "let the lightning bugs think we're part of the porch."

As twilight deepens, the light show begins in earnest. They rise from the garden like slow sparks, these bioluminescent benedictions, their patterns telling stories only summer nights can translate. The younger kids press their palms against their legs to keep from reaching out to catch them, having learned that the best way to love something is sometimes just to let it shine.

Grandma Lilly rocks slowly, her silver hair catching the last light like a halo. She remembers counting these same lights with her own grandmother, back when the porch was new and the world seemed simpler. "Every summer has its own song," she says softly, "and lightning bugs are the notes that write it."

The counting lasts exactly thirty minutes—measured by the old Seth Thomas mantel clock visible through the front window. When the last chime echoes across the yard, numbers are shared in whispers: "Forty-three." "Sixty-seven!" "Eighty-two this evening." They're recorded in a leather-bound journal that's documented every summer evening's count since 1962.

But the numbers aren't really the point. It's about gathering darkness and family light, about teaching children that patience reveals magic, about passing down the art of sitting still enough to see beauty unfold. It's about remembering that some things can't be rushed or captured—they can only be witnessed and cherished.

Later, when the lightning bugs have finished their evening dance and the kids have been tucked into bed, Grandma Lilly sits alone on her porch. She doesn't need the journal to remember summers when the counts reached into the hundreds, or the drought years when they dipped to single digits. Every number tells a story; every summer adds its verse to the family's testament of light.

"Some folks measure their lives in years," she says to the night air, her voice soft as a prayer. "We measure ours in lightning bug summers." And in the darkness, another tiny light rises from her garden, adding one more blessing to the count.

5

Stained Glass Morning

At 7:42 every morning, give or take a minute depending on the season, God paints Hope Baptist Church with liquid light. That's when the sun reaches just the right angle to pour through the east window—the one the congregation calls Amazing Grace—and transforms the simple country sanctuary into something close to heaven.

The window itself isn't particularly grand, not like those soaring Gothic masterpieces in city churches. Installed in 1923 by a traveling artisan whose name has been lost to time, it depicts a simple scene: a shepherd leading his flock beside still waters. But when that morning light strikes it just so, something miraculous happens.

Miss Eleanor, who's played the piano at Hope Baptist for sixty-three years, arrives early every morning to witness this daily resurrection of color. "The light comes through in layers," she explains, her voice soft with reverence. "First the blues, like dawn breaking over Galilee. Then the golds and ambers start their slow dance across the pews, turning ordinary pine into something precious. Finally, the deep purples and crimsons flow down the center aisle like royal robes."

For exactly twelve minutes, the morning sun transforms the humble sanctuary. The light paints shifting patterns on the whitewashed walls, turns dust motes into floating diamonds, and bathes everything in colors that seem to come from some heavenly palette. Even the old hymnals in their racks catch fragments of glory, their worn covers briefly blazing like burnished gold.

The congregation has never installed electric lights in the window, despite suggestions from visiting preachers. "Can't improve on God's timing," Deacon Johnson always says. They did, however, adjust their early Wednesday morning prayer meeting to coincide with this daily display of grace. Now the small group that gathers to pray finds their amens punctuated by heaven's own light show.

Some say it's just physics—angles and refraction, wavelengths and weather. But those who've sat in those well-worn pews while the light pours through know better. They've seen how the colors find the exact spot where someone sits grieving, how the light seems to linger longest where it's needed most.

Miss Eleanor keeps a small notebook where she records special moments: the morning when a rainbow settled like a halo around old Mr. Thompson the day before he passed, the shaft of golden light that touched the baptismal font

just as baby Grace was being dedicated, the crimson glow
that warmed the altar during revival week.

"People talk about seeing the light," she says, closing the
piano keys as the colors fade to ordinary morning. "But
sometimes the light sees us, finds us right where we are, and
reminds us that glory isn't just something that happens in
heaven. Sometimes it sneaks into country churches at 7:42
in the morning, just to make sure we don't forget how to
wonder."

6

The Lighthouse Keeper's Daughter

S arah Mitchell can tell you the exact moment when the St. Simons lighthouse beam cuts through evening fog—not by looking at her watch, but by feeling it in her bones. Growing up in the keeper's quarters taught her to measure life by the rhythm of light and shadow, by the predictable sweep of that great eye watching over the Georgia coast.

"The lighthouse isn't just a building," she says, running weathered fingers along the original brass handrail. "It's more like a heartbeat. Once you've lived with it long enough, it becomes part of your own pulse." At seventy-three, she's the last person alive who can remember what it was like when keeping the light was a sacred duty passed down through generations, not just a job for park service employees.

Her father was the last civilian keeper before automation changed everything in 1953. She remembers watch-

ing him climb those 129 steps every evening, no matter
the weather, to make sure the light stayed true. "Daddy
used to say, 'Ships might have radar and radio now, but
there's nothing more faithful than a beam of light cutting
through darkness.'"

The keeper's quarters still stand proud beside the tower,
though tourists now walk where Sarah once played. She
remembers her mother's herb garden beneath the kitchen
window, the way sheets on the clothesline would snap
like sails in the sea breeze, how every room moved to the
rhythm of the beam sweeping past the windows—three
seconds of light, three seconds of shadow, through every
night of her childhood.

These days, she volunteers as a docent, sharing stories
with visitors who can't quite imagine what it was like to
live in the constant company of light and shadow. She
tells them about hurricane nights when the beam seemed
to hold back the darkness by sheer force of will, about
summer evenings when moths danced in its path like stars
come down to earth, about the way her father would polish the brass until it shone like captured sunlight.

"People ask if it bothered me, living with that light
sweeping through my bedroom every night," she says,
looking up at the tower that still stands sentinel over her
memories. "But how do you explain that it was like being
rocked to sleep by light itself? Three seconds bright, three
seconds dark—as regular as a heartbeat, as faithful as a

prayer."

The lighthouse still sends its beam out over the sound, automated now but no less vigilant. And every evening, just as the sun settles into the marsh, Sarah walks the grounds of her childhood home. She doesn't need the 129 steps anymore to know the light is true—she carries its rhythm in her heart, where a keeper's daughter always knows the way home.

7

Morning Light at Andalusia

First light at Flannery O'Connor's Andalusia farm doesn't just arrive—it unfolds like one of her stories, revealing its mysteries layer by layer. The sun begins its daily manuscript across the old dairy barn's weathered boards, touching each crack and splinter until the whole structure glows like burnished scripture.

Regina, the last of the farm's peacocks, used to greet these dawns with raucous ceremony, her calls echoing across the pond where mist rises like incense from dark waters. Though she's long gone now, morning visitors swear they sometimes hear phantom peacock songs in the first light's golden hours, as if O'Connor's beloved birds left their voices behind to keep telling the farm's stories.

"Miss Flannery would sit right there," says Margaret Anne, the property's caretaker, pointing to the front porch where the author wrote in the cool of morning. "She'd watch the light change everything it touched, turning ordinary Georgia clay into something biblical." The worn wooden chair still faces east, as if waiting for another story to arrive with the dawn.

The morning light moves with deliberate grace across the grounds, touching each element of the farm like a priest giving blessing. It catches in the window panes of the main house, transforms the climbing roses into stained glass, and finally reaches the small room where O'Connor crafted her fierce and beautiful tales of grace arriving in unexpected ways.

Even now, decades after her passing, Andalusia holds its morning light differently than other places. Perhaps it's because O'Connor herself wrote so often about illumination—both divine and mundane—or perhaps it's simply that some places become sacred through the weight of attention paid to ordinary moments.

The old water tower casts its shadow across the cattle field where O'Connor's mother once ran dairy cows. Morning glories open their purple faces to the light, climbing the same fences that contained the author's beloved peacocks. Everything here seems both ordinary and extraordinary, like her stories—mundane details transformed by careful attention into moments of revelation.

"People come looking for ghosts," Margaret Anne says, watching the sun climb above the tree line. "But what they find instead is light—the same light Miss Flannery wrote by, the same Georgia morning that inspired her to see grace in all things, even the difficult ones." She pauses, listening to a whip-poor-will's last calls. "Some mornings, if you're quiet enough, you can almost hear her typewriter clicking away, telling stories about how grace catches us all, ready or not."

The sun climbs higher, burning away the last of dawn's mysteries. But for those who know how to look, how to wait in the quiet of morning, Andalusia still offers its daily revelation: that grace, like morning light, arrives whether we're watching for it or not, transforming everything it touches into something holy, something true.

8

Christmas Eve Luminaries

In Covington, Georgia, Christmas Eve arrives one paper bag at a time. By noon, they line every sidewalk and driveway around the square—simple brown bags, each containing a cup of sand and a single candle. Come dusk, these humble materials will transform the town into something that makes even the most hurried soul pause and remember what holy means.

The tradition began in 1963 with Sarah Beth Anderson's grief. Her son James didn't come home that Christmas, his helicopter lost somewhere in Vietnam. She lined their walkway with twelve luminaries—one for each month he'd been gone—and sat vigil through that long December night. By the next Christmas Eve, every house on Maple Street had joined her vigil. Now, sixty years later, the entire town glows with thousands of these small lights of remembrance and hope.

"It's not about the lights themselves," explains Tom Anderson, Sarah Beth's grandson, as he helps neighborhood children fold down the tops of paper bags. "It's about making a path for grace to follow home." The preparation itself has become ritual—families gathering to fill bags with sand, children learning the careful art of folding perfect cuffs, older folks sharing stories of Christmas Eves past.

At exactly 5:30, as the winter sun surrenders to evening, the lighting begins. It starts at the old courthouse, where the mayor lights the first candle from the eternal flame that burns for the county's veterans. From there, light spreads through town like a whispered prayer. Neighbors pass flame to flame, street to street, until the entire town glows with earthbound stars.

The transformation is remarkable. Simple streets become pathways of light. Regular folks become keepers of the flame. Children who helped fill bags now walk the luminaria-lined sidewalks with wide eyes, understanding perhaps for the first time that ordinary things—paper bags, sand, candlelight—can become extraordinary through the alchemy of shared purpose and remembered love.

"Mama always said the lights were for James," Tom continues, watching his own grandchildren carefully light each candle. "But they're really for all of us—for everyone trying to find their way home on a dark night, for everyone holding onto hope when the world seems dim."

As night deepens, carolers move through the streets,

their voices carrying on the winter air. People who normally rush from place to place now stroll slowly, speaking in hushed tones, as if they've entered some sacred space. In a way, they have. These lights transform the familiar streets into something holy—not through grandeur, but through the simple act of remembering, of lighting one small candle against the darkness.

By midnight, some candles will have flickered out, while others burn steady and strong. But that's part of the beauty too—this reminder that light, like life itself, is both precious and fleeting. Yet every year, on Christmas Eve, the people of Covington gather again to light the way home, carrying on Sarah Beth's vigil of hope, one paper bag, one candle, one small light at a time.

9

The Light She Left Burning

Every Southern mama knows there's more than one way to say "I love you." For ours, it was that porch light burning faithful as a lighthouse through every dark Georgia night. No matter how late we came home—from football practice, first dates, or midnight fishing—that light waited, holding back the darkness like her own hand cupped around a flame.

It wasn't just any light. It was the one by the front door, under the ceiling fan where carpenter bees tried to drill homes each spring. The glass globe had a chip on one side from the time Tommy's baseball went astray, but Mama never replaced it. "That chip," she'd say, "helps me recognize my own light from down the road."

Three boys could get into plenty of trouble, and Lord knows we did. But that light was Mama's way of saying she believed in second chances, in finding your way back, in the power of home to heal whatever the world had bruised. It burned through summer storms and winter frost, through teenage arguments and slammed doors, through all the growing pains three rowdy boys could muster.

Some nights, coming home late, we'd see it from the end of our dirt road—a golden beacon promising warm kitchen smells, fresh sheets, and forgiveness for whatever hour the clock showed. Even now, decades later, I can close my eyes and see it: that steady glow cutting through pine-scented darkness, drawing us home like moths to the only flame that mattered.

Mama never lectured about curfews or staying out too late. She didn't have to. That light spoke volumes—about worry wrapped in trust, about love that burns steady even when tested, about a mother's heart keeping vigil through the dark hours. It was her silent sermon, her luminous prayer, her way of reaching into the night to guide her boys home.

Years have passed. We've all got porch lights of our own now, burning for our own children. But none quite glows like Mama's did. Because wrapped in that simple light was everything we needed to know about love—that it waits, that it watches, that it welcomes you home no matter how far you've wandered.

That old chip in the glass is long gone, but the light still burns. Different bulb, same love. Same mama, same message: "Come home safe. I'm waiting. I love you." Sometimes the simplest light casts the longest shadow of grace.

10

The Light of the World

In the fellowship hall of New Hope Baptist, Miss Beatrice tends to the ancient oil lamp that's graced every Christmas Eve service since 1889. "It's not about the lamp," she says, polishing the brass until it gleams like morning. "It's about what it represents—how one small light can push back all that darkness."

Each Christmas Eve, as twilight settles over the red clay hills of North Georgia, the congregation gathers for what they call the Passing of the Light. Miss Beatrice, keeper of traditions and church histories, lights the old lamp first. From its flame, she lights the pastor's candle, and from there, light spreads through the sanctuary like grace made visible, person to person, flame to flame, until two hundred candles transform the simple country church into something that feels remarkably like glory.

The tradition started with Miss Beatrice's great-grandmother, Sarah, who carried that very lamp through Sherman's march, hiding it in a well when the army passed.

"She believed," Miss Beatrice explains, smoothing her apron, "that as long as she could keep one light burning, hope wouldn't die." That lamp has lit every dark night since—through wars and depressions, through storms that took the steeple and floods that reached the pews.

Tonight, as she prepares for the service, Miss Beatrice remembers all the faces she's seen in candlelight over her seventy-eight years—babies being dedicated, young couples exchanging vows, old saints saying their last goodbyes. Each flame connects them all, a chain of light stretching back through generations of faithful souls who understood that darkness doesn't stand a chance when people share their light.

"Jesus said we're the light of the world," she says, adjusting the wick just so. "But He didn't mean for us to shine alone. That's why we pass the light, because grace, like flame, only grows stronger when it's shared." She pauses, watching the flame dance in the polished brass. "And Lord knows, this old world needs all the light it can get."

Soon the sanctuary will fill, and the ancient lamp will once again kindle a sea of flames. In that holy moment between darkness and light, between the world as it is and the world as it could be, Miss Beatrice will see what her great-grandmother knew—that hope, like light, can't be destroyed. It can only be passed on, burning brighter with each hand that tends it, with each heart that carries it forward into the darkness.

11

Lantern and Legacy

Every evening at dusk, Harold McPherson climbs the wooden steps of Folkston's train-watching platform, carrying a brass railroad lantern that's older than his seventy-eight years. The ritual draws little attention from the tourists who gather to watch the endless parade of CSX freight trains passing through Georgia's "Funnel"—where most of Florida's rail traffic converges. But that lantern holds more history than all the steel giants thundering past.

"This was my daddy's light," Harold says, setting the lantern carefully on its dedicated post. "Before that, it belonged to my grandfather, who started working the Folkston line in 1918." He touches the worn brass like a priest handling sacred vessels. "Back then, every railman's light had its own signature swing—a language of light that could tell you who was working the yard just by how they moved their lantern."

The lantern's glow seems different from modern

lights—warmer, more alive somehow. Its flame dances behind glass that's grown cloudy with age, casting shadows that seem to speak of steam engines and midnight runs, of signal crews and track walkers who used these lights to hold back southern nights.

Harold remembers watching his father polish this same lantern every Sunday afternoon, telling stories about nights when this light was the only thing standing between safe passage and disaster. "Daddy used to say a railroad man's lantern was like his word—it had to be clear, steady, and true." He adjusts the wick with practiced fingers; a motion repeated so many times it's become something like prayer.

These days, the lantern serves more as symbol than necessity. Modern railroads run on electronics and satellites, not handheld lights and human signals. But Harold keeps the tradition alive, lighting this beacon every evening as trains rumble past. Engineers know to look for it—some even answer with two short whistle blasts, acknowledging this small flame that connects present to past.

"People ask why I still do this," Harold says, watching the lantern's glow reflect off passing rail cars. "I tell them it's not about needing the light anymore. It's about remembering that before all these modern signals, it was just people with lanterns, helping each other find the way home through the dark."

As night settles over Folkston's rails, the lantern burns

steady and true, just as it has for over a century. In its light, you can almost see the ghosts of railroad men past, swinging their lights in that ancient code of safety and fellowship. Some legacies, it seems, are best passed down in light.

12

First Light at Cumberland

F irst light on Cumberland Island arrives like a whispered prayer. The sun hasn't cleared the Atlantic horizon yet, but already its promise paints the sky in shades no artist could capture. Through the maritime forest's canopy, past gnarled live oaks draped in Spanish moss, the wild horses emerge from dawn mist like memories taking shape.

"The horses know when first light comes," says Miss Eleanor James, whose grandmother cooked for the Carnegies when they still ruled this island paradise. "They've been keeping this appointment since before any of us were here to witness it." She stands at the edge of the dunes; her bare feet pressed into sand still cool from night's retreat.

The mare appears first, dark mane catching the earliest rays. Behind her, a foal steps delicately through sea oats bending with morning dew. They move like spirits through the growing light, their hooves barely leaving prints in the dampened sand. These aren't the worked-tired horses of the mainland—these are descendants of Spanish bloodlines, carrying themselves with the pride of creatures who've never worn a saddle.

As the sun finally breaches the horizon, light spills across the beach like liquid gold. The dunes cast long shadows westward, creating a landscape of light and dark that changes with each passing minute. Sea birds wheel overhead, their wings catching fire in the new day's glow, their cries mixing with the eternal rhythm of surf meeting shore.

"My grandmother used to say that God practices painting the world every morning on Cumberland," Eleanor muses, watching the light transform everything it touches. "Said He gets it perfect here before moving on to the rest of creation." The rising sun proves her point, turning ordinary beach morning into extraordinary theater—Spanish moss becomes silver lace, ancient oak limbs become bronze sculptures, and even the oyster shells scattered along the tide line sparkle like scattered diamonds.

The horses move parallel to the shoreline now, their shadows stretching long across wet sand. They pay no mind to the few early risers watching from a respectful distance. This is their time, their ritual, passed down through generations of island-born foals who've never known any world but this one where wild still means something.

First light on Cumberland doesn't just illuminate—it reveals. It shows us what this barrier island has always been: a place where wild beauty still rules, where horses still run free, and where every morning brings its own kind of resurrection. As the day brightens toward ordinary time, the horses fade back into the maritime forest, leaving only hoofprints in the sand to prove they weren't just dreams born of dawn's first light.

13

The Light He Left Burning

Remembering Sapelo

The morning sun still rises over Sapelo's marsh grass just as it has for centuries, turning dew into diamonds, setting the spartina ablaze with golden light. The old lighthouse still stands sentinel, its red brick tower a testament to time and tide, watching over an island where memory now mingles with morning mist.

That October Saturday started like any other festival day—the air rich with the promise of friendship, fellowship, and celebration of Gullah-Geechee heritage. The marsh grass whispered ancient stories on the breeze, and longtime friends gathered as they had for years, their laughter echoing across Doboy Sound.

Among them was a soul whose love for this island ran as deep as the tidal creeks that lace through its salt marshes. He understood Sapelo's magic—how it exists suspended between sea and sky, between past and present, between the everyday world and something more eternal. Like so many others who cherished this place, he came to celebrate its unique culture, its enduring spirit, and its ability to keep old ways alive in a changing world.

The tragedy that followed reminds us that even the most sacred places aren't immune to sorrow. But on Sapelo, grief transforms like the turning tide. Here, where descendants of enslaved people maintained their dignity and culture through centuries of challenge, loss becomes legacy, and memory becomes mission.

Now, when the morning sun touches the marsh grass, it illuminates more than just dew. It shines on the strength of a community that has faced countless storms yet continues to preserve its heritage. It highlights the resilience of an island people who understand that love for a place, and for each other, runs deeper than any tragedy.

Those who knew him speak of how he embodied the spirit of Sapelo itself—graceful, strong, rooted in tradition yet reaching toward tomorrow. His legacy lives on in every sunrise that gilds these waters, in every story shared on front porches, and in every child who learns the old ways and carries them forward.

The ferry still makes its daily crossings, carrying those who understand that Sapelo isn't just a destination—it's a testimony. To visit now is to become part of an ongoing story of resilience, remembrance, and renewal. It's to understand that some lights never truly fade; they just find new ways to shine.

In the evening, when the sun sets behind the lighthouse and the marsh grass turns to silver in the gloaming, you can almost hear the island whispering its eternal truth: that love, like light, finds its way through the darkest night, guiding us home to the places and people that make our hearts whole.

We remember. We celebrate. We continue. Because that's what Sapelo and my friend teach us to do.

[Note: This piece aims to honor without sensationalizing, to remember while respecting privacy, and to celebrate the enduring spirit of both the person and the place.]

14

The Window Watcher

Miss Ruby's front window has been lit every night since 1958, casting its gentle glow across Bradford Street in the heart of small-town Georgia. Just as her mother did before her, she keeps that light burning from dusk until dawn—not for herself, but for anyone who might need its quiet comfort in the dark hours.

"Mama started it during the war," she explains, adjusting the old hurricane lamp that's held pride of place in that window for over six decades. "Said every soldier's mama was keeping a light on somewhere, so she'd keep one burning here for all of them." The tradition continued long after the war ended, becoming something larger than its origins—a beacon of consistency in an ever-changing world.

From her perch behind that glowing window, Miss Ruby has witnessed more of the town's story than any history book could hold. She's seen teenagers walking home from Friday night football games, their shadows stretching long under streetlamps. She's watched young couples steal their first kisses, thinking no one could see them in the evening's soft embrace. She's observed the midnight wanderers, the early risers, the lost souls seeking direction—all of them somehow comforted by that steady light.

"People ask why I don't put in one of those automatic timers," she says, striking a match to light the lamp as evening approaches. "But there's something about doing it by hand that matters. It's like saying to the night, 'I'm here. I'm watching. You're not alone.'"

The lamp itself is nothing special—just brass and glass, worn smooth by years of handling. But its light has guided more than one troubled soul home. The local police officer mentions how he uses it as a landmark during his night patrols. The paper carrier knows it means coffee and conversation await if he arrives while Miss Ruby's making breakfast. Even the town's teenagers know it as a safe harbor when parties go wrong, or dates turn sour.

At eighty-four, Miss Ruby keeps her vigil with the same faithfulness that defined her mother's generation. She understands that some traditions are really promises kept, that some lights do more than illuminate—they remind us that someone cares enough to keep the darkness at bay.

"Mama used to say that hope is just light with a purpose," she reflects, watching the flame catch and steady behind the glass. "I reckon that's why we keep this window lit. Not because anyone asked us to, but because everyone needs to know there's still light in the world, still someone watching, still a way home."

15

Tybee's Three Lights

From his weathered deck on the north end of Tybee Island, Captain Jimmy MacPherson can read the lighthouse beacons like other folks read their morning paper. Each light has its own signature, its own story, its own way of piercing the coastal darkness. "Three lights," he says, pointing toward the horizon. "Three different ways of saying 'This is the way home.'"

The main lighthouse—proud, tall, and steady—sends out its pattern like a heartbeat: one-two-three, pause, one-two-three. "That's the grandmother," Jimmy explains, his voice carrying the salt of sixty years on these waters. "She's been guiding ships home since 1867, never missed a night's work." The black and white tower stands sentinel over the island, its pattern as faithful as sunrise.

The range lights, working in tandem from their separate towers, create a different language altogether. When aligned properly, they form a single beam that guides ships safely through the channel. "Those are the dancing sisters,"

Jimmy says with a knowing smile. "Have to watch them both to get the true message. One without the other tells only half the story."

Each pattern speaks to something deeper than navigation. The main light's steady rhythm reminds old salts like Jimmy of simpler times, when finding your way home meant trusting in beacons tended by dedicated keepers. The range lights' partnership speaks to the importance of harmony, of things working together toward a common purpose.

"Young folks today got their GPS and radar," Jimmy muses, watching the lights paint patterns across the darkening water. "But there's something about these old lights that technology can't replace. Maybe it's knowing that these same beams guided your grandfather's grandfather home, or maybe it's just the comfort of seeing something steady in an unsteady world."

The patterns continue their ancient dance across the waves—three different lights, three different rhythms, all speaking the same essential truth: here is safety, here is harbor, here is home. For those who know how to read them, they're more than just navigational aids. They're reminders that some things remain constant, that some traditions are worth preserving, that some lights never lose their power to guide us home.

"People ask why we still need these lights," Jimmy says, his eyes reflecting the beacons' glow. "I tell them it's not about need anymore. It's about remembering that before all our modern conveniences, it was just light and faith that brought us home through the dark. Still is, if you think about it right."

16

The Dark Corner's Dawn

In South Carolina's "Dark Corner," where mountain mist clings to ancient ridges like a lover's goodbye, dawn arrives with deliberate grace. Here, in this remote stretch of the Blue Ridge foothills—once known for moonshine and mysteries—first light reveals what darkness kept hidden through the night.

Jesse McAbee stands on his grandfather's porch, third cup of coffee growing cold in his weathered hands. At seventy-two, he's watched more mountain dawns than he can count, each one a revelation of what his great-grandmother called "God's own watercolors." The sun hasn't crested Caesar's Head yet, but already the sky is transforming from velvet black to indigo to something there's no proper name for.

"Folks who don't live here wonder why we call it the Dark Corner," Jesse says, his voice carrying the melody of these hills. "Truth is, it's not about the dark at all—it's about what happens when light finds its way into places that have kept secrets for generations."

The mist begins to lift as day approaches, revealing patchwork fields and weathered barns that have watched over this land since before the Civil War. Each morning brings its own theater of light—sometimes golden rays pierce through fog like divine fingers touching earth, other times the whole valley fills with a pearly glow that makes the ordinary seem sacred.

"My grandfather used to say that dawn in the Dark Corner shows you everything you need to know about redemption," Jesse reflects, watching color seep into the landscape. "How light doesn't judge what it touches—just transforms it. How even the darkest hollow eventually sees morning."

These hills hold stories as deep as their shadows—tales of resistance and survival, of bootleggers and revenue men, of families holding onto traditions while the world rushed toward tomorrow. But in this morning light, those stories seem less about darkness and more about the persistent courage of people who kept their own ways in their own time.

First light touches the old still site where Jesse's grandfather once turned corn into liquid lightning. Now it's just a collection of rust and memories, but the morning sun gilds it like a monument to ingenuity and grit. "Some folks are ashamed of that history," Jesse says. "But in the right light, you can see how it was really about independence, about making your own way when the world didn't leave you many choices."

The Dark Corner earned its name in harder times, but dawn reveals its true nature—not a place of darkness at all, but a sanctuary where light and shadow dance their eternal dance, where morning mist makes magic of the mundane, and where every sunrise reminds us that transformation is always possible.

"People think darkness defines this place," Jesse says as the sun finally crests the ridge, setting the whole valley ablaze with promise. "But we who live here know better. It's not about the dark at all—it's about the light that follows, sure as grace follows prayer."

17

Candlemakers of Savannah

In a narrow brick workshop off Factors Walk, where river mist mingles with history's whispers, Sarah Beth Chandler practices an art older than Savannah itself. Her hands move with inherited grace, dipping wicks into melted beeswax with the same rhythm her grandmother used, and her grandmother before her—four generations of women who've lit Savannah's darkness with handcrafted flame.

"Every candle tells a story," she says, gesturing to the rows of tapers hanging like stalactites from wooden racks. "These hurricane candles? They're made the same way colonists made them—thick enough to burn through coastal storms, shaped to fit the old brass holders still found in Savannah's historic homes." The workshop smells of beeswax and history, of tradition melted down and poured into new forms.

The Chandler women (yes, that's their real name—"God's own joke," Sarah Beth calls it) have been

Savannah's candlemakers since 1842. They've lit cere-
monies that marked the city's highest celebrations and
deepest sorrows. Their candles have burned in St. John's
Cathedral, illuminated nights at Bonaventure Cemetery,
and guided countless couples through candlelit courtships
in the squares.

"People think it's just about wax and wicks," she explains, testing a flame's strength. "But it's really about continuity—about keeping something authentic in a world
that seems to prefer the artificial." Her candles contain no
paraffin, no synthetic scents. Just beeswax from local hives,
cotton wicks hand-twisted on rainy afternoons, and the
accumulated wisdom of generations.

Sarah Beth works in the old way—by feel and flame
rather than thermometers and timers. She knows when the
wax is right by its sheen, judges a candle's quality by the
way its light dances. "Mama used to say a proper candle
flame should move like a lady dancing a minuet—graceful,
steady, but with just a hint of wildness."

Each morning, she opens the shop's wooden shutters
to let river light spill across worn floorboards that her
great-grandmother's skirts once swept. The tools of her
trade hang in their appointed places—dipping frames,
wick winders, moulds that have shaped countless candles.
But the real inheritance isn't in the equipment—it's in the
knowing, in the rhythm, in the understanding that some
things are worth preserving.

"In an age of electric everything," she says, trimming a wick with practiced precision, "there's still something about real candlelight that speaks to the soul. Maybe because it's alive—dancing, breathing, reminding us that light isn't just illumination. It's a living connection to all the lights that came before."

18

Stadium Lights and Fireflies

On Friday nights in Fitzgerald, Georgia, two kinds of lights dance together—the bright industrial glare of stadium lights and the soft, sacred glow of late summer fireflies. As the Purple Hurricanes take the field, these different lights tell the story of a small town where football isn't just a game, but a weekly reunion of souls.

Old Coach Williams, retired now but still claiming his seat in the press box, remembers when they first installed those lights back in '73. "Everyone pitched in," he says, his voice carrying the gravel of forty seasons of sideline calls. "Farmers brought their tractors, merchants donated materials, and every able body in town helped raise those poles. We didn't just build a lighted field—we built a gathering place for light itself."

The fireflies arrive as twilight softens into evening, rising from the tall grass beyond the end zone like nature's own pep rally. They dance through the warm September air, tiny benedictions floating past the stadium lights' harsh glare. Some folks say they're the spirits of every touchdown ever scored here, still celebrating in the gathering dark.

"My daddy used to tell me that fireflies are God's way of teaching us that the smallest lights matter," says Maria Hernandez, who's been running the concession stand for twenty-three years. "Even with those big lights blazing, you can still see every little lightning bug doing its part to light up the night."

The mixture of lights creates something magical—industrial brightness spilling across the field while natural light performs its ancient dance around the edges. In the stands, generations of families sit together, their faces illuminated by both kinds of light. Children chase fireflies during halftime, their mason jars glowing like captured stars, while grandparents tell stories of games played beneath these same lights decades ago.

Sometimes, in the fourth quarter, when the score is close and tension rides the cooling night air, you might see a firefly drift across the end zone just as a receiver stretches for a pass. For that brief moment, two kinds of glory merge—the electric brilliance of stadium lights catching a championship play, and nature's own luminescence offering its quiet approval.

"It's not just about football," Coach Williams reflects, watching another Friday night unfold beneath this dance of lights. "It's about community, about tradition, about the way some lights bring us together while others remind us that magic still exists in ordinary places."

As the game clock winds down and families begin their slow exit into the evening, both kinds of light remain—one steady and strong, lighting the way to parking lots and waiting cars, the other floating free and wild, reminding us that some Friday nights are made of equal parts electricity and enchantment.

19

The Light in Room 204

For forty-three years, Miss Katherine Bennett has kept the old hurricane lamp burning in Room 204 of Marshland Elementary. Not because the fluorescent lights don't work, but because some kinds of illumination reach deeper than mere brightness. That brass lamp, rescued from her grandmother's attic, has watched over four decades of young minds learning to shine.

"It started my first-year teaching," she explains, adjusting the lamp's antique chimney with practiced care. "A little boy was terrified of storms, and we had a bad one rolling in. Something about that warm, steady light calmed him—reminded him of his grandma's house, he said. After that, the lamp stayed."

The lamp has witnessed generations of children discover the magic of reading, the wonder of science, the joy of understanding something for the first time. Its gentle glow has comforted anxious test-takers, illuminated impromptu story times during power outages, and created what Miss Katherine calls "circles of courage" where shy students found their voices.

"Modern education's all about smart boards and tablets now," she says, her voice carrying the warmth of countless story times. "But there's something about this old light that helps children feel safe enough to learn, brave enough to try, steady enough to grow."

The lamp has become more than just classroom decor—it's a character in countless stories. When former students visit, often with their own children in tow, they always ask about "Miss Katherine's light." They remember how it made Monday mornings feel like coming home, how its glow seemed to make hard things easier, how it turned an ordinary classroom into a place where magic might happen.

Tommy Jenkins, Class of '92, told me he got through multiplication tables by focusing on that lamp," she recalls, smiling at the memory. "Said as long as that light was burning, he knew he could figure it out eventually. He's a mathematics professor now."

Each morning, Miss Katherine arrives early to light the lamp, a ritual unchanged by decades. She touches its brass base, worn smooth by years of children's curious fingers, and remembers all the little lives it's helped illuminate—the struggling readers who became novelists, the anxious mathematicians who discovered elegance in equations, the quiet dreamers who found their voices in its gentle glow.

"People sometimes ask why I don't retire," she says, watching the flame dance behind its glass chimney. "But how do you retire from being the keeper of a light? Besides, every year brings new children who need to know that some lights never go out—they just keep burning, steady and true, showing the way forward."

In Room 204, where knowledge meets nurture and tradition meets tomorrow, Miss Katherine's lamp keeps its vigil. Not just a light in the darkness, but a beacon of continuity in a changing world—reminding us that the most important things we learn often come by the gentlest light.

20

Moonshine and Starlight

U p in Georgia's northern hills, where mountain laurel grows thick and creeks run cold and clear, old-timers still talk about nights when moonshine and starlight worked together to guide midnight commerce through secret paths. These weren't just tales of outlaws and revenue men—they were stories of survival, ingenuity, and a different kind of light showing the way home.

Jasper McCall, whose grandfather ran sugar through these hills during the Depression, sits on his cabin porch watching tonight's full moon paint the ridges silver. "Folk nowadays think moonshining was all about breaking laws," he says, his voice carrying the quiet authority of mountain wisdom. "But back then, it was about feeding families, keeping farms, holding onto land that'd been passed down since before the Revolution."

The same moon that illuminates his porch tonight once guided men carrying heavy loads through mountain passes, their footsteps silent as prayers. They learned to read the night sky like sailors read the sea—knowing when the moon would light their path and when starlight alone would have to suffice. Every shadow, every patch of brightness held meaning.

"Granddaddy used to say you could tell a man's character by how he moved through moonlight," Jasper recalls, watching shadows shift across his yard. "Said some walked like they were apologizing for existing, while others moved like they had an understanding with the night itself."

These hills hold countless stories of moonlit adventures—tales of men outrunning the law, of secret signals flashed between ridges, of stills hidden so deep in mountain hollows that only starlight ever found them. But they're also stories of communities supporting each other through hard times, of farmers turning corn into cash when crops wouldn't sell, of proud people finding ways to endure.

"The revenue men had their lights too," Jasper chuckles, remembering stories passed down through generations. "Big old flashlights that could cut through darkness like a knife. But they didn't know how to read the gentler lights—how moonshine on laurel leaves looks different from moonshine on pine, how starlight can show you safe paths if you know how to listen to it."

Today, these hills have changed. The old paths have grown over, the secret caves hold only memories, and legal distilleries make moonshine for tourists. But on nights like this, when the full moon rides high and stars pierce the velvet sky, you can almost hear the whispered stories these mountains keep.

"Some folks think darkness is the absence of light," Jasper muses, watching the moon cast tree shadows like lace across his yard. "But up here, we learned that darkness just shows you different kinds of light—the kind that guides you home when regular paths won't do, the kind that reminds you that sometimes the finest things happen by starlight."

21

Dawn's Early Light at Fort Pulaski

Every morning, just as the sun begins to paint the marsh grass gold, Sergeant James Monroe raises the flag at Fort Pulaski. The ritual hasn't changed since 1862—same pole, same dawn, same sacred purpose. Only the soldiers are different, and even they seem touched by the same light that watched over their predecessors more than a century and a half ago.

"You can feel them here in the early hours," Monroe says, his fingers running along the weathered halyard. "All those who stood this watch before." The morning mist rolls in from the Savannah River, wrapping around the fort's red brick walls like a soldier's cloak, waiting with him for dawn's arrival.

The fort holds its own kind of light—not just the sun's first rays catching on the morning dew, but the kind of light that comes from stories waiting to be remembered. These walls have witnessed war and peace, triumph, and surrender, all painted in the changing colors of countless Georgia dawns.

As the eastern sky begins to brighten, Monroe prepares the flag with practiced reverence. Every fold, every motion carries the weight of tradition. "People think it's just about raising a flag," he reflects, "but it's really about connecting with something larger than ourselves. When that first light hits the stars and stripes, it's touching the same flag design that flew here during the Civil War."

The ritual begins precisely twenty minutes before sunrise. Monroe's boots echo across the parade ground—the same ground where Union and Confederate soldiers once stood. The flag, carefully folded into its triangle of honor, waits to greet another dawn. Above, the sky transforms from indigo to lavender to rose, nature's own tribute to what's about to unfold.

As the sun crests the horizon, Monroe begins raising the flag. The morning light catches each stripe as it rises, turning red and white into flame and silver. Time seems to slow, as if history itself pauses to witness this daily resurrection of purpose and pride. The only sounds are the quiet whisper of marsh grass in the morning breeze and the gentle clicking of the halyard against the pole.

"Sometimes," Monroe says, watching the flag catch the freshening breeze, "you can almost hear the echoes—the drummer's call, the morning gun, the footsteps of sentries long gone. But mostly, you hear the silence, the kind of quiet that tells you you're part of something that started long before you and will continue long after."

The flag reaches full staff just as sunlight floods the parade ground. For a moment, it hangs still in the morning air, then slowly begins its dance with the coastal wind. Below, the fort's red bricks glow like embers in the dawn light, while above, the stars and stripes paint their own shadows across grounds that have seen nation divided and reunited.

This is more than just a military ceremony—it's a daily reminder that some traditions light our way forward by illuminating where we've been. As the sun climbs higher and the day begins in earnest, the flag continues its watch over the fort, just as it has since that first morning when dawn's early light revealed its stars still there.

22

Reflective Light in Art

Light never travels alone. Each beam carries stories, bouncing between surfaces, whispering secrets only artists truly hear. In Margaret Anne's sunlit studio, where morning spills through tall north-facing windows, canvases speak of reflection in both its forms—the physical dance of light and the deeper contemplation it inspires.

She stands before an unfinished painting of Forsyth fountain at dawn, where water drops catch fire and Spanish moss turns to silver. Her brush hovers, considering the next stroke that might capture that ephemeral moment when light touches water and learns to dance. This is what she calls "light's second journey"—the way it transforms after meeting the world.

The morning light streams across her workspace, casting long shadows that hold pools of secondary illumination, softer and more mysterious than direct beams. She studies how this reflected light reveals the truth about form, showing us that objects don't simply end at their shadows but continue around, like stories unfolding.

On her walls hang studies of light's endless conversation with the world—silver reflections off oyster shells, golden light bouncing between autumn leaves, the complex play of brilliance within crystal glasses. Each canvas demonstrates how reflected light adds depth and meaning to what might otherwise be flat shadow.

The most challenging reflections, she finds, are those in human eyes. Every portrait becomes a study of light twice transformed—once by the physical world, once by the spirit behind the gaze. She works now on a judge's portrait, trying to capture not just the light in his eyes but the weight of wisdom it carries.

As morning advances toward noon, the light in her studio shifts, creating new reflections and revealing new possibilities. She steps back from her easel, considering how to capture this moment's particular luminosity. Each reflection is unique, just as every moment of light holds its own truth, waiting to be understood and shared.

In the end, all art is about reflection—both the physical phenomenon and the contemplative act. Artists reflect what they see, what they feel, what they understand about the world. Sometimes, if they're very lucky, their work reflects something true enough to help others see their own light more clearly.

The day leans toward afternoon now, and Margaret Anne cleans her brushes as the light begins its westward journey. Tomorrow it will return, bringing new stories, new reflections, new truths to be captured on canvas. For now, she stands in the glow of her morning's work, surrounded by paintings that speak of light's endless dance with the world.

23

The Phosphorescent Sea

Some nights, when the moon plays hide-and-seek with clouds and the tide runs just right, the waters off Jekyll Island perform their own kind of magic. Like stars falling into the sea, tiny organisms create a light show that transforms ordinary waves into flowing silver, each splash becoming a shower of living sparks.

Miss Eleanor Davis has watched these waters for sixty summers. From her weathered beach chair, positioned just where the dunes meet the tide line, she's become a keeper of phosphorescent secrets. "The old-timers called it 'sea fire,'" she says, her voice carrying the soft lilt of coastal Georgia. "But I think it's more like the ocean sharing its dreams with us."

The phenomenon appears without warning—though Miss Eleanor swears she can sense it coming. "You need a dark night," she explains, "and water that feels like silk when it runs through your fingers." Tonight, as waves break against the shore, each one leaves a trail of blue-green light that lingers for precious seconds before fading back to darkness.

Local children have learned to watch for Miss Eleanor's beach chair on summer evenings. When they see her settling in with her thermos of sweet tea, they know magic might be coming. They gather around her like fireflies to a lamp, waiting for her signal. When she finally nods, their delighted squeals pierce the evening as they splash through illuminated surf, their footprints briefly glowing like lunar footsteps.

"My grandmother used to tell me that these lights were the souls of sailors finding their way home," she says, watching young feet kick up sparks in the shallow water. "Scientific folks call it bioluminescence, but I prefer to think of it as the sea sharing its joy."

The display changes with each wave. Sometimes it's just a gentle sparkle, like diamond dust scattered on black velvet. Other times, when the conditions are perfect, entire waves seem to catch fire, rolling toward shore like liquid moonlight. Schools of fish move through deeper water like underwater comets, their passage marked by trails of living light.

Miss Eleanor remembers the night sixty years ago when her father first showed her this marvel. "He said that some of God's finest work happens in the dark," she recalls, smiling at the memory. "Said it was to remind us that light doesn't always come from above—sometimes it wells up from within."

These illuminated nights have become part of Jekyll's unofficial calendar, marked not by dates but by tides and seasons, by the phase of the moon and the temperature of the water. Those who know how to read these signs gather on certain evenings, drawn by the possibility of witnessing the sea's luminous dance.

As tonight's show reaches its peak, Miss Eleanor watches a young girl standing at the water's edge, her face glowing with wonder as waves light up around her feet. "That's what these nights are really about," she says softly. "Not just the light in the water, but the light you can see in people's eyes when they witness something magical. Both kinds of light tell us the same thing—that wonder still exists in this world, if we just know where and when to look for it."

24

First Light at Tallulah Gorge

Two thousand feet deep and carved by ancient waters, Tallulah Gorge wakes up slowly. Dawn arrives here in layers, like a story being told one whisper at a time. First, there's just a softening of darkness above the rim, while the gorge floor still dreams in shadow. Then, as if God himself is dimming up the lights, the morning begins its slow descent into Georgia's deepest canyon.

Marcus Weatherford has watched this daily performance for thirty years from his perch on Inspiration Point. "Every morning tells a different story," he says, his voice barely carrying above the whisper of the falls. "Sometimes the mist rises up like spirits from the gorge floor, other times it settles in layers like a wedding cake made of clouds."

The first rays touch the eastern rim, turning bare rock to rose gold. Shadow still holds the western wall, creating a study in contrasts that photographers have tried to capture for generations. But as any local will tell you, Tallulah's light show can't be contained in a single frame—it's more like a symphony played in luminescence.

As sunlight continues its patient journey down the gorge walls, it reveals the face of the canyon piece by piece. Ancient gneiss sparkles with mica, while ribbons of quartz catch fire and seem to flow like frozen rivers of light. The massive rock faces, which appear gray and formidable in full day, briefly blush pink in these first moments of morning.

"The Cherokee called this place 'Ugunyi'—the place of the terrible noise," Marcus explains, nodding toward the falls that give the gorge its voice. "But in these early hours, before the day tourists arrive, you can hear something else too—the sound of light itself washing down these walls."

A pair of peregrine falcons, reintroduced to the gorge years ago, catch the morning thermals, their wings briefly gilded by sunrise as they dance their ancient sky ballet. Below them, the cascading waters of the falls begin to sparkle, transformed from their nighttime silver into ribbons of liquid gold.

The floor of the gorge is the last to receive the morning's blessing. Here, where the air stays cool and damp even in August, ferns unfurl in the strengthening light while trillium and wild orchids turn their faces toward the brightening sky. The morning sun, now fully risen above the rim, sends shafts of light through the mist like spotlights searching out nature's hidden treasures.

"People ask me why I come here every morning," Marcus says, watching the last shadows retreat from the gorge floor. "I tell them it's because no two dawns are ever the same. Just when you think you've seen every way light can paint these walls, every way shadow can dance with sunshine, the gorge shows you something new."

As the day brightens toward ordinary time, the magic of first light gradually fades. But for those who witnessed it, the memory lingers—of how darkness surrendered to dawn in layers, of how light filled an ancient canyon like water filling a cup, of how morning revealed, once again, that some places are sacred not despite their depths, but because of them.

25

The Light Painters of River Street

On Savannah's River Street, where cobblestones still whisper tales of cotton merchants and river captains, a different kind of artist gathers each morning. They come with easels and palettes, chasing what local painter Marie DuBois calls "the most elusive light in Georgia"—that magical moment when sunrise sets the Savannah River ablaze and transforms weathered brick into burning bronze.

"The light here is alive," Marie says, setting up her easel in front of an ancient warehouse. "It bounces between river and buildings, between sky and cobblestones, creating colors that don't exist anywhere else." Her brush hovers over the canvas, waiting for that precise moment when the sun crests the South Carolina shore and turns the river into liquid fire.

They call themselves the River Street Light Chasers—a loose fellowship of artists who've learned to read morning light like others read weather maps. Each has their favorite spot: Jerome claims the stairs near the Waving Girl statue, Sarah Anne sets up by the cotton exchange, and old Mr. Patterson hasn't missed a sunrise from his corner near Factor's Walk in twenty years.

"You've got exactly seventeen minutes," Mr. Patterson explains, his weathered hands moving quick strokes across his canvas. "That's how long the perfect light lasts—from when the sun first touches the river until it rises above the warehouse roofs. Seventeen minutes to catch glory."

The light here performs a daily ballet. First, it skips across the river in golden ripples. Then it catches the tops of the buildings, turning century-old brick into something almost translucent. Finally, it reaches the cobblestones, where each worn surface reflects the morning differently, creating a mosaic of light that changes with every step.

These painters have learned to work fast, to catch fleeting moments before they fade. Their canvases capture light in its many moods: the way it filters through ghost-gray Spanish moss, how it plays along the iron balconies, how it transforms puddles after a rain into mirrors of sky.

"Some folks think we're crazy," Marie says, her brush dancing across the canvas, "getting here before dawn, painting the same street day after day. But every morning shows us something new. The light never tells the same story twice."

They've become as much a part of River Street as the

cobblestones themselves. Restaurant workers heading to early shifts know them by name. Tour guides point them out to visitors. And their paintings, hanging in galleries along the river, tell the story of Savannah's light in all its moods and seasons.

As the sun climbs higher and tourists begin to appear, the Light Chasers pack up their easels, their canvases holding captured moments of dawn's brief glory. Tomorrow they'll return, ready again to paint the light that dances between river and stone, sky, and history—each artist adding their own verse to River Street's daily poem of light.

26

Light in the Okefenokee

Deep in Georgia's great swamp, where black water mirrors cypress knees and Spanish moss hangs like ancient memories, light behaves differently. It doesn't just illuminate—it transforms. Here, where water the color of strong tea reflects a cathedral ceiling of branches, every beam of light tells a story.

Morning arrives like a slow revelation. First light touches the tops of the cypress trees, their branches wearing crowns of golden moss. Then it begins its patient descent, filtering through layers of leaves and Spanish moss, creating what old-timers call "tree rain"—beams of light falling like liquid gold through the canopy.

The swamp mirrors this light show, its dark waters acting as nature's own reflecting pool. Every beam is doubled, creating a world where up and down become interchangeable, where light seems to come from both above and below. In these moments of dual light, everything seems to float between two worlds.

As day progresses, light plays different tricks. It catches in strands of spider silk strung between cypress knees, turns water droplets on pitcher plants into prisms, makes the wings of dragonflies flash like stained glass. Alligators bask in sunny spots, their scales turning to bronze in the warmth.

But it's the night lights that fuel the swamp's richest stories. When darkness falls, mysterious lights dance above the water, leading curious followers deeper into the swamp's embrace. Some say they're just swamp gas catching moonlight; others insist they're the lanterns of long-gone travelers still trying to find their way home.

The swamp keeps its own counsel about which stories to believe. A shaft of sunlight finds its way through the canopy, creating a perfect circle of gold on the dark water. These spotlights appear and vanish throughout the day, each one a temporary stage for the swamp's endless theater of light and shadow.

As evening approaches, the swamp begins its transition from one light show to another. The western sky turns to flame above the cypress tops, while the first stars begin to peek through gaps in the canopy. Soon the moon will rise, creating silver pathways across the black water, and the night chorus will begin their song.

In the Okefenokee, light isn't just about seeing—it's about believing. Whether it's the first golden rays of dawn touching cypress knees, the mysterious dance of swamp

lights in the darkness, or the way moonlight turns Spanish moss to silver lace, each illumination tells part of the
swamp's eternal story. And like the water that gives this
place its character, these lights run deep, holding mysteries
that even the oldest swamp families are still trying to understand.

27

Light Through Sugar Cane

In late October, when the Louisiana sun hangs low in the sky, it discovers secrets in the cane fields. Light doesn't just shine here—it sifts, it seeps, it transforms. Each stalk becomes a prism, turning ordinary evening light into something sacred.

Stand at the edge of a hundred acres of ripening cane just before sunset. Watch how the light changes from white to gold to amber, filtering through countless green-gold stalks that bow and wave in the autumn breeze. The whole field becomes a living cathedral, each row an aisle, each stalk a pillar holding up a ceiling of light.

When the wind moves through, the light seems to dance. Shadows and brightness play tag between the rows, creating patterns that shift and flow like water. The rustle of dry leaves provides nature's hymn, while the sweet smell of ripening cane hangs in the air like incense.

This is the time old-timers call "cane light"—that magical hour when sunlight turns each field into a chamber of liquid gold. From the ground, looking up through the stalks toward the setting sun, you can see how light breaks into countless beams, each one finding its own path through the dense growth. The effect is like looking through stained glass made of living things.

Sometimes a late butterfly will drift through these light-struck aisles, its wings catching the glow, turning it into a ember floating through streams of gold. Hawks hunting in the evening light cast shifting shadows across the luminous field, their silhouettes sliding over the cane like dark boats on a bright sea.

As the sun sinks lower, the show becomes even more spectacular. Light seems to pool at the base of the stalks, creating rivers of gold between the rows. The tops of the cane catch fire with the last rays, each tassel becoming a torch that burns without consuming. For a few precious minutes, the whole field seems to hold its breath, caught between day and night, between earth and sky.

This is more than just a daily light show—it's a reminder of how the ordinary can become extraordinary through the simple magic of light. These fields that represent generations of hard work, of planting and praying and harvesting, transform each evening into temples of natural light.

Soon the harvesters will come, and these cathedral aisles will fall to feed the mills. But for now, in this moment between work and rest, between summer and fall, the cane fields perform their daily miracle. They teach us how to capture light, how to break it into its component parts, how to turn it into something sweeter than itself—just as they've been doing since the first cane was planted in Louisiana soil.

28

Morning Light on Angel Oak

The first rays of dawn approach Angel Oak with reverence. They have to navigate carefully—through Spanish moss that hangs like ancient lace, between branches that reach farther than any tree has a right to reach, around limbs so heavy they rest their elbows on the earth. This is no ordinary tree, and this is no ordinary light.

Four hundred years of mornings have touched these branches, each dawn adding another ring of memory to the great oak's girth. Some branches stretch longer than seventy feet, creating their own horizons. Others dip down to touch the earth before rising again, as if the tree is trying to gather the ground into its embrace.

Dawn arrives in whispers. First, a pearly glow touches the highest branches, turning dew drops into constellations. Then light begins its slow dance through the canopy, creating shadows that tell stories no human tongue can translate. The Spanish moss catches the early rays and holds them, each strand becoming a fiber optic cable of golden light.

This is the hour when Angel Oak reveals its true nature. Shadows and light play across bark that has witnessed centuries of human drama—wars and peace, slavery and freedom, hurricanes and calm mornings just like this one. Each knot and furrow in its ancient trunk becomes more pronounced as the light strengthens, like lines on the face of a wise elder telling silent stories.

The tree creates its own atmosphere. As morning mist rises from the ground, it mingles with light filtering through the canopy, creating what locals call "angel breath"—a luminous fog that drifts between the massive branches like spirits of the past coming to pay their respects. This is when you understand why some call this tree a living cathedral.

Photographers have tried for generations to capture this moment, but Angel Oak's morning light show defies documentation. How do you photograph reverence? How do you capture the way light seems to pause as it touches bark that was already ancient when the Declaration of Independence was signed? Some things can only be witnessed, not recorded.

As the sun climbs higher, the light show changes but never diminishes. Shadows shift and dance across the ground like nature's sundial. Light finds new paths through the labyrinth of branches, illuminating different stories, different memories. The great oak holds it all—light and shadow, past and present, earth and sky—in its massive embrace.

This is more than just a tree catching morning light. This is a living temple where light itself comes to worship, where time moves more slowly, where the boundary between natural and supernatural blurs with each dawn. Stand here long enough and you begin to understand why the old ones believed trees could be sacred.

Soon the day tourists will arrive with their cameras and their chatter. But for now, in this space between night and day, Angel Oak performs its daily miracle. It teaches us how light can make the ancient new again, how shadow can reveal rather than conceal, how some places are sanctified not by human intention but by the simple act of surviving, of witnessing, of reaching ever upward toward the light.

29

The Lights on Brasstown Bald

At Georgia's highest point, where four states spread out below like a patchwork quilt, light behaves differently. Up here on Brasstown Bald, at 4,784 feet above the everyday world, dawn arrives first and darkness lingers last, painting the Blue Ridge Mountains in colors that exist nowhere else on Earth.

Morning comes as a slow explosion of light. First, a pearl-gray glow touches the eastern horizon while the valleys below still dream in darkness. Then color begins to seep into the world—pink, then gold, then a blue so pure it makes your heart ache. From this height, you can watch shadows retreat from the mountaintops like tide going out, leaving pools of light in their wake.

On rare winter mornings, when the peak rises above a sea of clouds, Brasstown becomes an island in the sky. Light skips across the cloud tops like stones across water, turning the ordinary into the sublime. Below, towns and valleys sleep under their blanket of mist while up here, light performs its daily miracle unwitnessed except by early hikers and the occasional deer.

Summer evenings bring their own kind of magic. As the sun sinks toward Tennessee, light seems to pool in the valleys like liquid gold. The shadows of mountains stretch across the landscape like great purple fingers, while every window in the towns below catches fire with reflected sunset. Up here, twilight lingers like a goodbye kiss, reluctant to leave this highest point in Georgia.

But it's the night lights that tell the most remarkable stories. On clear evenings, when the air has been scrubbed clean by afternoon thunderstorms, you can see the lights of Atlanta shimmer on the southern horizon like earthbound stars. Closer in, small towns sparkle in the valleys like fallen constellations, each one a collection of human dreams burning against the darkness.

Sometimes, during the deepest part of winter, the northern lights dance across these peaks—curtains of green and purple light rippling above the ancient mountains. These rare displays remind us that Brasstown Bald stands as Georgia's ambassador to the sky, our highest reaching into heaven's lowest, a place where earth and stars meet in sheets of shimmering light.

Through all the seasons, the observation tower keeps its vigil, its light a single steady star marking Georgia's ceiling. Around it, darkness and light perform their eternal dance, painting these mountains with shadows and glory, telling stories that can only be read from this height, in this air, at this meeting place of earth and sky.

Up here, you understand why the Cherokee considered these peaks sacred ground. Some places are holy not because humans declared them so, but because they stand as witnesses to the eternal dance of light and shadow, day and night, heaven and earth. Brasstown Bald is such a place—Georgia's highest altar, where light itself comes to worship.

30

Light Through Cathedral Live Oaks

When morning light filters through Savannah's cathedral of live oaks, time slows to a reverent whisper. Here, where ancient branches reach across streets like vaulted arches and Spanish moss hangs like nature's-stained glass, sunlight transforms from mere illumination into something holy.

The light arrives in layers. First, it touches the highest branches, turning moss-draped limbs into floating rivers of gold. Then it begins its patient descent, filtering through countless layers of leaves and moss, creating what locals call "tree light"—that peculiar luminescence that exists nowhere else but under these living cathedrals.

Stand at one end of any oak-lined street just after sunrise. Watch how the light breaks into countless beams as it passes through the canopy, each shaft of sunlight becoming its own sermon of radiance. The Spanish moss catches these beams and holds them, turning from gray to silver to gold, creating a chandelier effect that stretches for blocks.

When the morning breeze moves through, the whole cathedral comes alive. Light and shadow dance between the branches, creating patterns that shift and flow like water. The rustle of leaves provides nature's hymn, while the moss sways like slow-motion waterfalls of light. This is when you understand why the first settlers kept these trees—they weren't just saving shade, they were preserving sanctuaries.

Each oak creates its own light signature. Some filter sunlight into distinct beams, like spotlight through clerestory windows. Others diffuse it into a general glow that seems to come from everywhere and nowhere at once. The oldest trees, with branches that dip and rise like frozen waves, create entire chambers of light and shadow.

In these green-gold spaces, everyday moments become sacred. A child chasing a leaf through bars of sunlight becomes a dancer in nature's spotlight. An early morning jogger passes through alternating bands of light and shadow, each stride marking time in this cathedral of trees. Even the squirrels seem to move with more grace as they navigate through their backlit kingdom.

As the sun climbs higher, the show changes but never diminishes. Shadows shift across the ground like nature's sundial. Light finds new paths through the labyrinth of branches, illuminating different stories, different moments. The oaks hold it all—light and shadow, past and present, earth and sky—in their massive embrace.

This is more than just trees catching morning light. This is nature's own Notre Dame, where light itself comes to worship, where time moves more slowly, where the boundary between natural and divine blurs with each dawn. Stand here long enough and you begin to understand why humans first built cathedrals—they were trying to recreate this very thing, this dance of light through reaching branches, this sense of the sacred made visible through illumination.

Soon the day will fully arrive, with its traffic and tourists and ordinary time. But for now, in this space between night and day, Savannah's cathedral of oaks performs its daily miracle. It teaches us how light can make the ancient new again, how shadow can reveal rather than conceal, how some places are sanctified not by human intention but by the simple act of surviving, of witnessing, of reaching ever upward toward the light.

31

Light Through Antebellum Glass

I n the heart of Savannah's Historic District, where time moves like molasses in January, the morning sun finds stories in old window glass that modern panes can never tell. Each bubble, wave, and imperfection in antebellum glass transforms ordinary sunlight into something extraordinary—rainbow-kissed moments that connect us to generations past.

Stand in the parlor of the Owens-Thomas House just as dawn breaks. Watch how light bends through glass that was hand-blown before the Civil War, each pane slightly rippled like the surface of a gentle stream. These aren't the flaws of poor craftsmanship—they're the signatures of human breath, preserved in sand and time, each distortion telling its own story of the artisan who shaped it.

The morning light enters these old windows differently than it enters modern ones. It doesn't just pass through; it dances, it splits, it plays. Tiny air bubbles trapped in the glass two centuries ago become prisms, casting dozens of tiny rainbows across heart pine floors. These are the same rainbow patterns that delighted children in hoop skirts and kept housemaids company as they went about their morning duties.

In certain angles of early light, you can see the subtle waves in the glass—evidence of how the molten material once flowed like water before cooling into transparency. These waves turn sunbeams into fluid art, creating patterns that move across walls and floors as the sun makes its daily journey. Each window becomes a kind of lens, transforming ordinary daylight into something that feels almost alive.

Old glass remembers. The slight green tint in the upper panes comes from iron impurities in the sand used to make them—sand probably scooped from a Carolina beach before Andrew Jackson was president. When summer light shines through, it carries that same green memory into modern times, painting the present with colors from the past.

Even the dust that settles on these ancient panes plays a part in the light show. Motes drift through slanted morning beams like tiny stars, each one catching fire for a moment before floating on. In these suspended particles, you can almost see the passage of time itself, marked out in points of light.

But it's the late afternoon sun that draws the finest art

from antebellum glass. As day draws toward evening, light stretches across rooms like honey poured from a jar, picking up all the subtle distortions in the old panes. Shadows take on unexpected shapes, light pools in unexpected places, and for a few precious moments, the ordinary world becomes extraordinary through the lens of history.

These windows have watched nearly two hundred years of sunrises. They've seen war and peace, feast and famine, joy and sorrow, each moment filtered through their imperfect perfection. Today's light passes through the same ripples and bubbles that once bent the light that fell on Civil War generals, on enslaved people dreaming of freedom, on ladies in morning dress, on children playing marble games on polished floors.

In an age of precision-made glass, these old windows remind us that imperfection can be beautiful, that flaws can create magic, that light itself can be a kind of memory. They teach us that sometimes the most perfect view of the present comes through a lens shaped by the past.

As twilight approaches and the last light fades from these historic panes, they hold one final secret: in the right light, at the right moment, you can still see fingerprints pressed into the glass by long-ago craftsmen. These ghostly whorls and loops, preserved in silica and time, remind us that everything we build, everything we create, carries something of ourselves into the future—even if it's just the way we teach light to dance.

32

Gullah Lantern Ways

In the Sea Islands that string like pearls along the coasts of Georgia and South Carolina, light tells stories in whispers. Here, where Gullah traditions still pulse strong as tide rhythms, old ways of lighting the darkness carry wisdom passed down through generations of hands that knew how to make light speak.

Sweet grass baskets hold hurricane lanterns whose flames dance to ancient rhythms. These aren't just sources of illumination—they're beacons of cultural memory, each one carefully placed to guide spirits home or ward off haints, each flame a testament to traditions older than slavery, newer than tomorrow's sunrise.

"De light gotta know which way home be," Mama Rosa always said, setting her lantern in the east-facing window. The flame, steady as a lighthouse beam, throws patterns through the hand-blown glass onto worn wooden floors. These shadows speak their own language, one taught by African ancestors who knew that light was more than mere brightness—it was a way to keep stories alive, to guide both the living and the dead.

Blue bottle trees catch morning light like captured stars, their cobalt glass turning sunbeams into protective spirits. Each bottle holds not just light but memory—the deep blue of African skies, the flash of Caribbean waters, the color of freedom dreams. When evening comes, lantern light catches in these bottles, creating a dance of blue shadows that locals say keeps evil from crossing the threshold.

On nights when the moon rides high over marsh grass, you might still see lanterns moving through island paths—not the harsh glare of electric lights, but the gentle glow of tradition. These lights mark the way to praise houses where rings shout still thunder against wooden floors, where voices rise in rhythms carried across oceans, where light and shadow play their eternal dance of remembrance and hope.

The old ones teach that proper light placement matters more than brightness. A lantern in the wrong spot might confuse the ancestors; one in the right place lights the way for blessings. Even today, in modern homes with electric switches, you'll find hurricane lamps placed just so—by doors, at crossroads, near water—keeping watch like silent guardians of tradition.

Some nights, when salt marsh meets starlight and distant shrimping boats string their working lights across the horizon like a pearl necklace, you can still hear the old stories. They tell of lights that led people to freedom, of lanterns that spoke in code, of flames that kept faith burning through the darkest nights of history.

These Gullah lantern ways aren't relics—they're living traditions that still light paths through darkness, still guard doorways, still guide spirits home. Each flame carries echoes of Africa, whispers of survival, promises of continuation. In a world of harsh fluorescent glare and LED efficiency, these gentle lights remind us that sometimes the old ways of illumination carry the brightest wisdom.

As evening settles over the Sea Islands like a prayer shawl, lanterns begin their nightly vigil. Their light speaks in the old tongue, telling stories of remembrance and resistance, of survival and celebration, of a people who knew that the right kind of light could bridge worlds, connect generations, and keep cultural memory burning bright as any flame.

33

Theater Lights on Broughton

When the marquee lights of Savannah's Historic District flicker to life each evening, Broughton Street transforms into a ribbon of memories. The Lucas Theatre's Art Deco glow mingles with the warm sparkle of the Trustees, each bulb a tiny star in an urban constellation that's been lighting up Georgia nights since vaudeville's heyday.

First come the ghost lights—single bulbs left burning center stage in both theaters, keeping company with the spirits of performers past. These solitary sentinels have never missed a night's watch since the curtains first rose. Stage managers still climb the worn steps each morning to replace them, carrying on a tradition as old as theater itself.

As twilight deepens, the marquees begin their nightly performance. The Lucas, restored to its 1921 splendor, casts a warm amber glow that turns sidewalk strollers into silhouetted actors in their own evening drama. Each bulb in its elaborate display was placed to match archival photographs, creating the same light show that dazzled movie-goers when "talkies" were still new.

The Trustees Theater's vertical sign pierces the evening sky like an exclamation point of light, its red neon reflecting off the windows of neighboring shops just as it did when Bobby Darin once graced its stage. Between these theatrical bookends, Broughton Street becomes a corridor of illuminated history, where modern LED displays share space with vintage neon, and yesterday's elegance meets today's energy.

Inside these grand houses, stage lights tell their own stories. Ancient Fresnel lenses, their glass ridged like fingerprints, still catch and shape light the way they did when George Gershwin played here. Modern instruments share the rails with spotlights that once followed Buddy Holly across the stage, each beam carrying its own echo of applause.

The follow spots still dance their ballet during performances, operated by hands that understand the poetry of illumination. These beams know how to kiss a soprano's face just so, how to build drama with shadow, how to make a dancer seem to float on air. They're choreographed as carefully as any performance they illuminate.

Between shows, work lights reveal the theaters' secrets—the hemp rope systems still used to fly scenery, the old-growth pine stage floors burnished by countless soft-shoe routines, the ghost light standing sentinel until the next performance begins. These utilitarian beams show the bones of theatrical magic, the infrastructure of dreams.

But it's during the blue hour—that magical moment between sunset and full dark—when Broughton Street's theaters truly come alive. As day yields to dusk, the marquees begin their gradual brightening, each bulb warming up like an orchestra tuning. The street becomes a stage set for evening's performance, where every passerby plays their part in the ongoing story of Southern nights.

These aren't just lights—they're keepers of memories, markers of culture, beacons calling us to gather in the dark and share in something larger than ourselves. They remind us that in the South, even our illumination has stories to tell, if we just take the time to watch the show.

34

The Lighthouse Women

In the keeper's quarters of St. Simons Light, where salt air meets brass polish, the women who kept Georgia's coast safe left their stories in logbook entries and fingerprints on wind-worn windowpanes. While history often shines its spotlight on the men who manned our lighthouses, it was often their wives, daughters, and sisters who kept the lights burning through the darkest storms.

Consider Sarah Moore, who took over St. Simons Light when influenza claimed her husband in 1905. She would climb the 129 steps each evening, just as twilight painted the marsh in amber hues. Her logbook entries tell of nights when storms raged so fierce she had to tie herself to the tower railing to change the light's mantles. Yet her handwriting never wavered—steady as the beam she maintained.

Along our coast, these women knew the weight of responsibility measured in ships saved and lives preserved. They learned to read weather in the way light bent through

morning haze, to gauge storms by how the beacon reflected off approaching clouds. Their children grew up
knowing that darkness was not an option, that the light
must always prevail.

At Tybee Light, Elizabeth Saffold raised three children
alone while keeping the great lens turning. She would cook
dinner with one eye on the sky, knowing exactly when
the light needed tending. Her youngest daughter recalled
watching her mother polish the brass until it shone like
captured sunshine, teaching her that lighthouse keeping
wasn't just a job—it was a sacred trust.

These women mastered the complex dance of maintaining Fresnel lenses, each prism requiring precise cleaning
to bend light into life-saving beams. They learned to feel
when the mechanism needed adjustment, to hear the difference between the normal song of turning gears and the
whisper of something amiss. Their hands knew every inch
of their lights, every quirk of ancient machinery.

Night after night, they would wind the weights that
kept the lights turning, haul the oil that kept them burning, trim the wicks that kept them bright. During hurricanes, they stayed in their towers while others fled inland,
knowing that those were the nights when their light meant
the difference between life and death for sailors fighting
angry seas.

Some, like Mary Miller of Little Cumberland Light,
kept their vigils in almost complete isolation. She would

stand in her tower at dawn, watching the light fade as morning painted the Atlantic in pearl and rose. Her only company was the rhythm of waves and the crying of gulls—yet her light never failed, her watch never faltered.

Their legacy lives on in the automated beacons that still guide ships along our coast. Though no one climbs the stairs with oil cans now, no one polishes brass until it gleams, these lights still carry the dedication of the women who once kept them. Each flash echoes their commitment; each beam carries their stories across the waves.

In the keeper's house on St. Simons, where Sarah Moore once watched storms approach across the sound, modern visitors can still feel the presence of these remarkable women. Their spirit lingers in worn stair treads, in handwritten log entries, in the very quality of light that still streams through old windows.

They were more than lighthouse keepers—they were guardians of hope, keepers of safety, priestesses of illumination. Their story is written in light across our coastal waters, in beams that still reach out into darkness, saying what they've always said: here is safety, here is harbor, here is home.

35

Midnight at Mercer

In Monterey Square, where Spanish moss drapes like silver in moonlight, Mercer House stands as a dark guardian of Savannah's secrets. When the midnight hour approaches and tourists have long since returned to their beds, the house performs its nightly transformation beneath the moon's careful attention.

The Italian marble steps, worn smooth by generations of footsteps, catch moonbeams and hold them like precious stones. Each classical column becomes a study in light and shadow—Corinthian capitals throwing complex patterns across the brick façade, while moonlight traces every curve and scroll as if mapping the house's memories.

High above, dormer windows reflect stellar light like knowing eyes. These same panes once witnessed the comings and goings of Jim Williams, whose story became entwined with the house's darker fame. On nights when the moon is full, these windows seem to hold their own illumination, as if the house itself is keeping watch over its square.

The wrought iron balconies cast latticed shadows across the brick—geometric ghosts that shift with the moon's passage. Each metalwork pattern becomes more pronounced in this ethereal light, telling stories in shadows that daylight never reveals. The massive front door, with its brass fittings polished to a subtle glow, stands like a portal between present and past.

Around midnight, when the live oaks are full of moonlight and the fountain in Monterey Square whispers its eternal song, the house seems most alive. Shadows pool in corners where garden paths meet brick walls, while moonlight silvers the camellias that still bloom in Jim's carefully planned gardens. The night air carries the scent of Confederate jasmine, its white flowers luminous as stars fallen to earth.

The house plays tricks with light at this hour. Moonbeams catch in window glass, creating brief flashes that might be reflections—or might be something else entirely. The carved stone details along the roofline throw shadows that seem to move of their own accord, while the deep porches hold darkness like secrets.

Even the old carriage house, scene of the infamous shooting that inspired "Midnight in the Garden of Good and Evil," has its own midnight personality. Moonlight traces the outline of its doors and windows, while shadows gather in its corners like whispered conversations. The brick path leading to it becomes a silver ribbon in the night, each paver outlined in lunar light.

On nights when clouds drift across the moon, the house seems to breathe with the changing light. Shadows advance and retreat across its face like waves on a shore, while brief moments of brightness reveal details usually hidden in day's harsher illumination. The old brick glows with a warmth that only moonlight can reveal, each handmade block telling its own story in subtle variations of shadow.

Local ghost tour guides will tell you that midnight is when the house is most likely to reveal its secrets. But perhaps the real magic lies not in what might appear, but in what the moonlight reveals about the house itself—its elegance, its mysteries, its enduring presence as anchor and guardian of one of Savannah's most beautiful squares.

As midnight deepens toward morning, Mercer House maintains its dignified vigil. The moon continues its arc across the sky, painting the house in ever-changing patterns of light and shadow. Here, in these quiet hours, the house reminds us that some places are most alive when the rest of the world sleeps, and that moonlight sometimes reveals truths that sunshine never knows.

36

Dawn's Promise at Providence Canyon

In the heart of southwest Georgia, where iron-rich soil bleeds red in morning light, Providence Canyon awakens like a watercolor painting coming to life. First light touches the rim, turning exposed clay into bands of amber, crimson, and rose—nature's own Georgia O'Keeffe, painting with sunbeams and mineral-stained soil.

They call it Georgia's Little Grand Canyon, but that name doesn't capture the intimacy of dawn here. As night retreats, the canyon reveals itself in layers, each stratum telling a different story in a different shade. White kaolin glows like fresh snow, while iron oxide burns orange-red, and manganese leaves purple shadows in the deepening clefts.

Morning mist often clings to the canyon floor, creating an ethereal sea from which the painted walls rise like islands. These fog banks catch first light and hold it, turning from pearl to pink to gold as the sun climbs higher.

Through gaps in the mist, ancient pine roots reach out from canyon walls like gnarled fingers frozen in their endless search for soil.

The erosion that carved these canyons—begun by simple farming practices in the 1800s—continues its artistry each dawn. Water seeps from the walls where clay meets sand, catching morning light in countless tiny mirrors. These natural prisms scatter sunbeams across the canyon faces, creating momentary rainbows that dance across the striated walls.

As the sun rises higher, shadows retreat up the canyon walls like tide going out, revealing new colors with each passing minute. What looked purple in first light becomes burgundy, what was pink deepens to coral, what seemed white takes on hints of cream and yellow. The canyon's colors shift like a mood ring responding to the warming air.

Photographers call it "the golden hour," but here it might better be named "the painted hour." This is when the canyon's famous red walls truly come alive, glowing as if lit from within. The interplay of light and shadow creates depth that no camera can quite capture, turning geological accident into natural art gallery.

Down on the canyon floor, where small streams still carve tomorrow's patterns, early light filters through overhead trees, creating shifting patterns on water and sand. Deer prints from night wanderings still show clearly in damp clay, each track holding a tiny pool of reflected sky. The morning chorus of birds echoes off the walls, their songs becoming part of the canyon's dawn symphony.

Local wisdom says every sunrise here is different, shaped by season, weather, and the ever-changing canvas of the canyon walls. Winter mornings paint everything in stark contrasts and long shadows. Spring brings wildflowers to soften the clay edges with dots of color. Summer dawns arrive with their own humidity-softened light, while autumn cloaks the rim in golden leaves that catch and reflect the rising sun.

This is more than just another Georgia sunrise. It's a daily revelation of how destruction can create beauty, how erosion can reveal art, how morning light can transform mere dirt into cathedral walls. Each dawn reminds us that sometimes the most beautiful things come from unexpected places—even from mistakes long past.

As full daylight finally reaches the canyon floor, the magic of dawn softens into the steady light of day. But the promise remains, carried in the continuing trickle of water, in the slow dance of shadow and light across mineral-painted walls—tomorrow's dawn will create new art, reveal new colors, tell new stories in this unexpected gallery carved from Georgia clay.

37

Light on Cotton

When morning breaks over a modern Georgia cotton field, it reveals a landscape that bridges centuries. First light catches in the fiber the same way it did when cotton was king—each boll becoming a prism, turning sunrise into something sacreWd. The rows stretch toward the horizon like waves frozen in white-tipped stillness, waiting for day to paint them gold.

Dawn arrives differently here than anywhere else. It begins as a pearl-gray whisper above the fields, then spreads like water across the cotton tops. Each plant holds the light differently—some bolls scatter it like tiny mirrors, others cradle it like cups of luminescence. The dew, not yet burned away by day's heat, turns each fiber into a light catcher, creating a field of countless stars anchored to Georgia soil.

Modern harvesting machines wait at field's edge like sleeping giants, their metal skins gradually warming in the growing light. They're a far cry from the hand-picking days, but the cotton they tend still catches morning light the same way—still transforms ordinary sunbeams into something that speaks of both beauty and survival.

Mid-morning light reveals the geometry of modern cotton farming—laser-leveled rows that stretch ruler-straight toward the horizon, GPS-guided precision that would amaze the sharecroppers of yesterday. Yet when the light hits just right, slanting through the plants and catching in the open bolls, time seems to fold back on itself. For a moment, it's hard to tell if you're seeing 2025 or 1925.

There's a particular quality to the light in cotton fields just before harvest. The plants, heavy with opened bolls, create their own kind of illumination. Sunlight bounces between the rows, reflects off the white fiber, creates a glow that seems to hover just above the plants like a blessing. Old-timers call it "cotton light"—a luminescence unique to these fields in these moments.

Late afternoon brings its own magic. The low sun turns cotton fields into seas of gold and white, each row casting long shadows that create strips of alternate light and darkness. The cotton seems to catch fire in this light, each boll becoming a tiny flame in a field of natural candlelight. It's the kind of light that painters dream about and photographers chase—when the ordinary becomes extraordinary through simple illumination.

Even the machinery takes on different character in evening light. Massive pickers cast shadows like prehistoric creatures across the fields, while their metal surfaces reflect the sunset in unexpected ways. They become part of the light show, their bulk softened by the same golden hour that turns cotton to fire.

But it's the cotton itself that remains the star of this daily light show. Whether it's catching first dawn, holding noon's brightness, or reflecting sunset's final glory, cotton transforms light in ways no other crop can match. Each boll becomes a lens, each field a living lesson in how light behaves when caught by nature's own fiber optics.

As day fades to dusk, the cotton fields perform one final trick of light. In the blue hour between sunset and full dark, the white bolls seem to hold onto the last remnants of day. They glow with a subtle luminescence that makes the fields look like they're covered in phosphorescent foam, each plant a wave caught between day and night.

This is more than just agriculture in afternoon light—it's a daily reminder of how our past connects to our present, how something as simple as sunlight on cotton can bridge generations. The light that paints these modern fields is the same light that witnessed the whole history of Southern cotton, from slavery through sharecropping to today's mechanical harvest. It holds all these stories in its golden beams, telling them anew each day to anyone who takes the time to watch the light dance across the fields.

38

Fire Tower Nights

Sixty feet above the North Georgia forest, where pine tops whisper ancient songs to passing clouds, the last of the manned fire towers keeps its lonely vigil. Here, darkness arrives differently than it does on the ground—in layers, like ink settling through water, while the western sky still holds onto day's final embers.

Miss Ruby has watched these transitions for twenty-three years from her perch in the Tower Five cab. "Every night tells its own story," she says, adjusting the radio that connects her to civilization. Her small domain, a 7x7 glass house in the sky, transforms into a observatory of light and shadow as day surrenders to dusk.

The first shift in light comes when the sun dips below Lookout Mountain. Long shadows reach across the valleys like purple fingers, while ridgelines still catch golden light. This is when the forest reveals its secrets—when smoke from a campfire can be distinguished from evening ground fog, when the last light catches in dewdrops on spider webs that connect tower legs to earth.

Inside the cab, Miss Ruby's world is defined by the Osborne Fire Finder—a brass and steel compass that's been helping spotters locate fires since 1920. As darkness deepens, she lights the small lamp that illuminates this ancient instrument. The flame reflects off the glass windows, creating a small universe of light suspended between earth and sky.

"Night watch is different now than it used to be," she explains, gesturing toward distant lights that mark civilization's advance. When she first started, the darkness was nearly complete—now suburban glows create false dawns on the horizon. Still, on moonless nights, the stars wheel overhead with a clarity found only at elevation, their light bright enough to cast shadows.

The tower's own lights tell stories too. A red beacon on top blinks its warning to low-flying aircraft, while small safety lights outline the steep stairs that spiral down into darkness. On stormy nights, lightning turns the whole forest into day for brief, brilliant moments, and the tower's metal frame hums with electric possibility.

Summer brings the light shows she loves best—fireflies rising from the forest like sparks from an invisible fire, their lights dancing between earth and stars. "Sometimes," she says, "you can't tell where the lightning bugs end and the stars begin." The morse code of their flashing creates conversations only night watchers understand.

But it's the unexpected lights that keep her vigilant. A flash where no flash should be, a glow that doesn't match the usual patterns of civilization or nature. These are what she watches for, ready to triangulate their position on her fire finder, to radio coordinates that will guide rangers through the darkness to whatever burns in her forest.

The night holds other lights too—the green glow of her instrument panel, the flash of deer eyes caught in her spotlight during perimeter checks, the occasional meteor painting brief silver lines across the black sky. Each one adds to the complex dance of darkness and illumination that makes up her nightwatch.

As midnight approaches, when the forest below has become a dark sea dotted with occasional lights like ships on an invisible ocean, Miss Ruby begins her log entries. Her small lamp catches the brass of the fire finder, the glass of the windows, creating a cocoon of warm light in the vast darkness. Up here, between earth and sky, she keeps her vigil—one of the last human links in a chain of watchers that stretches back to when these mountains were young.

In an age of satellites and infrared sensors, there's still something irreplaceable about having human eyes scanning the night, about knowing that someone watches from above while the world sleeps below. As long as there are forests to protect and fires to spot, there will be a need for these towers, these lights, these watchers in the sky.

39

Garden Lights of Bellingrath

I n Mobile's famous gardens, where azaleas once reigned as spring queens, winter nights now hold their own magic. As twilight deepens over Bellingrath, thousands of tiny lights awaken like earthbound stars, transforming fifteen acres of Southern grace into a luminous wonderland that Walter and Bessie Bellingrath could never have imagined.

The Great Lawn unfolds first, its century-old live oaks dressed in cascading curtains of light. Each massive branch wears a mantle of tiny white bulbs that mirror the Spanish moss by day—nature and artifice combining to create something entirely new. The effect is like watching a constellation map come to life, as if the stars themselves decided to dance closer to earth.

Along the Mirror Lake, lights perform a different kind of magic. Reflections double every gleaming strand, creating the illusion of infinite depth in the dark water. Japanese maples, their bare winter branches outlined in ruby lights, seem to float between two worlds—one reaching toward heaven, its twin extending into watery depths below.

The Rose Garden, though sleeping in winter's embrace, finds new life in illumination. Each dormant bush wears a net of tiny lights that recreates the geometry of summer blooms. The formal paths between them become rivers of soft light, leading visitors through a maze of luminous architecture where every turn reveals a new pattern, a fresh combination of light and shadow.

In the Asian American Garden, paper lanterns cast their glow across still ponds where koi sleep beneath dark waters. Here, the lighting designers showed particular restraint—each fixture placed to suggest rather than overwhelm, creating scenes that might have stepped from a Japanese woodblock print. The red bridge, outlined in white lights, seems to float on darkness.

The Magic Christmas in Lights display has evolved over decades, but some elements remain constant. The Cathedral of Light, where visitors walk through a tunnel of pure illumination, still draws gasps of wonder. The effect is like stepping into a corridor of stars, each tiny bulb contributing to an overwhelming sense of being surrounded by light itself.

But it's in the quieter corners where the true magic happens. Down garden paths where camellias bloom in winter darkness, subtle lighting reveals their perfect flowers as if caught in eternal moonlight. Near the Boathouse, strings of lights reflect off Mobile Bay, their glow mixing with distant stars until it's hard to tell which lights belong to earth and which to heaven.

Conservation plays its part in this modern light show. LED technology has replaced the power-hungry bulbs of yesteryear, but the warm glow remains unchanged. Each fixture is carefully placed to highlight both natural and architectural features while protecting the gardens' delicate ecosystem. Even the night-blooming cereus gets its moment of glory, spotlit on those rare evenings when its flowers unfold.

The original iron gates, through which countless visitors have passed since 1932, now stand transformed by light into portals of wonder. Their intricate scrollwork, outlined in tiny white bulbs, creates a filigree of light that seems to float in darkness. It's a fitting entrance to this illuminated paradise, where Southern horticultural tradition meets modern lighting artistry.

As night deepens and the last visitors depart, the gardens hold their luminous vigil. Security guards making their rounds speak of how different the light show looks in empty gardens—more intimate somehow, as if the lights are performing only for the sleeping flowers and ancient oaks. Each path tells its own story in patterns of light and shadow; each corner holds its own small miracle of illumination.

Here, in this merger of natural beauty and human artistry, Bellingrath reminds us that gardens need not sleep through winter nights. Instead, they can transform into something equally magical—a place where light itself becomes the flower, where darkness serves as soil, and where wonder blooms in all seasons.

40

The Last Gas Lamps

I n Charleston's oldest quarters, where cobblestones still whisper horse-drawn tales, the soft glow of gas lamps creates pools of living light that electricity can never quite match. These eternal flames, cupped in centuries-old glass, paint the nighttime streets in shades of amber that modern bulbs have forgotten how to produce.

Each evening, Michael Warfield makes his rounds with the same deliberate pace his grandfather used, carrying tools unchanged since Charleston's earliest days of gas lighting. "Every lamp has its own personality," he says, adjusting a flame that dances too high. "Some are temperamental as cats, others steady as old dogs, but they all need the same gentle touch."

The ritual begins at dusk. Each lamp must be checked, each mantle inspected, each glass pane cleaned of salt air's persistent film. These aren't museum pieces kept burning for tourists' cameras—they're working lights that have illuminated these streets through hurricanes and history, through war and peace, through countless nights of Charleston's endless stories.

The light they cast is different from anything modern technology can replicate. It's alive, for one thing—always moving, always dancing, creating shadows that seem to breathe. On foggy nights, each lamp creates its own aurora, a halo of diffused light that turns mist into magic. The soft glow catches in wrought iron balconies, makes the Confederate jasmine gleam like scattered stars, transforms ordinary evening air into something from another time.

Charleston's commitment to preserving these lamps goes beyond mere historical preservation. It's about maintaining a particular quality of light that shaped how this city grew, how its architecture developed, how its residents learned to see their world after dark. Under gas light, brick takes on a warmth that electricity can't capture, while stucco walls become canvas for dancing shadows that tell stories in light.

The mechanics of each lamp remain surprisingly simple: gas flows through pipes laid generations ago, feeds mantles that glow with the same steady light that guided residents home before the modern era. Each flame burns with a consistency that hasn't changed since the first lamp was lit in these narrow streets.

But it's not just about maintaining antique technology. These lamps create an atmosphere that defines Charleston's historic district after dark. Their gentle glow softens hard edges, turns familiar corners into mysterious passages, makes even routine evening walks feel like steps into the past. Under gas light, the present moment seems to blur around the edges, allowing past and future to mingle in pools of living light.

As midnight approaches and most of the city sleeps, the gas lamps keep their quiet vigil. Their light catches in windowpanes that remember centuries of stories, reflects off garden walls that survived nature's worst tempests, turns ordinary rain puddles into mirrors of history. Each flame burns as testament to a time when light itself was precious, when darkness was held at bay one lamp at a time.

In an age of instant illumination, these last gas lamps remind us that some things are worth preserving not because they're efficient, but because they're beautiful. They teach us that sometimes the old ways of holding back the night carry wisdom that technology can't improve upon—that some kinds of light can only come from fire, and some kinds of magic only happen in the dancing shadows of flames that have burned, unbroken, for generations.

41

River Light on the Chattahoochee

First light touches the Chattahoochee like a hesitant lover, fingers of dawn reaching through morning mist to stroke the ancient waters. Here, where Cherokee feet once traced paths along muddy banks, the river plays an endless game with sunlight, sometimes catching it like hammered gold, sometimes breaking it into a thousand dancing pieces.

Morning reveals the river's many moods. In the narrows, where water tumbles over rocks worn smooth as pottery, light fragments into bright shards that flash like broken mirrors. Deeper pools hold light differently—gathering it, transforming it into liquid amber before releasing it in slow, rolling waves. Above it all, river birch leaves flutter like silver coins in the strengthening day.

By mid-morning, when the mist burns away, the river shows its true colors. Through clear shallows, sunlight reaches to the bottom, turning river stones into underwater jewels—amber, jade, and smoky quartz. Bass move through these lit waters like living shadows, while overhead, osprey watch for silver flashes that betray their prey.

Summer afternoons bring their own light show. Sun-warmed rocks break the current into bright ribbons, each ripple catching light differently. Children tubing down the gentle rapids squeal as they pass through patches of sunshine and shadow, their laughter echoing off the water like skipped stones. The river seems to hold light in layers—some on the surface, some in its depths, some caught in the eternal dance between air and water.

When storms approach, the river's relationship with light turns dramatic. Dark clouds create deep purple shadows that race across the water, while breaks in the clouds send spotlights stabbing down to turn patches of river into brilliant silver. Lightning transforms everything for split seconds, making the familiar river strange and new with each flash.

Evening brings softer magic. As day fades, the river seems reluctant to let go of light. Long after shadows claim the banks, the water holds onto a pearl-gray luminescence. Mayflies dance above the surface like bits of floating starlight, while fish rise to meet them, creating ripples that catch the last gleams of day.

But it's during the blue hour—that magical time between sunset and true night—when the river performs its finest tricks with light. The water takes on colors that exist nowhere else in nature, deep blues that seem to glow from within, while the sky's last light creates a mirror so perfect it's hard to tell where water ends and heaven begins.

On full moon nights, the river becomes a ribbon of liquid silver winding through the Georgia darkness. Moonlight catches every ripple, turning the surface into hammered metal, while deeper water holds the light and sends it back changed, somehow more mysterious for its journey through the depths.

This is more than just light on water—it's the story of how the Chattahoochee has reflected our history back to us through centuries. From Native American fishermen to mill workers, from baptisms to summer swimmers, from power plants to paddlers, the river's light show has been a constant witness to the South's unfolding story.

The river moves ever onward, never the same twice, yet always itself. And the light moves with it, dancing on its surface, diving into its depths, telling stories that only water can tell. Here, where Georgia's ancient heart still beats in flowing water, light and river join in an endless dance that began before our time and will continue long after we're gone.

42

Midnight at Jekyll Club

In the velvet darkness of a Georgia coastal night, the Jekyll Island Club Hotel rises like a Victorian ghost ship anchored in time. Moonlight plays architect here after midnight, rebuilding the Gilded Age masterpiece in shadows and silver, transforming wood and brick into something that exists between memory and dream.

The grand turret catches moonlight first, its weathervane turning starlight into brief flashes of brilliance against the ink-black sky. Below, hundreds of windows—each original to the 1886 structure—reflect and hold light differently. Some seem to glow from within, as if the ghosts of Rockefellers and Vanderbilts still keep their lamps burning in eternal leisure.

The wraparound porch, with its forest of white columns, creates a play of light and shadow that changes with each passing cloud. Rocking chairs, empty now, cast elongated shadows across weathered planks—each shadow telling its own story of countless summer nights, of cigars and brandy, of deals that shaped a nation's fortune.

Spanish moss transforms in this light, becoming silver curtains that dance in the salt breeze. The ancient live oaks that frame the Club seem to hold pockets of darkness in their massive limbs, while allowing thin streams of moonlight to paint patterns on the manicured lawn below. These patterns shift and change like the shadows of long-ago croquet games played by America's aristocracy.

The fountain in the courtyard takes on a different personality after midnight. Water becomes liquid moonlight, each droplet catching and holding a bit of stellar fire before falling back into the dark pool below. The sound of water meeting water creates a gentle music that seems to belong specifically to this hour, to this place.

Around the grand entrance, where horses and carriages once delivered the world's wealthiest families, shadow and light play games with perception. Architectural details emerge from darkness only to disappear again—a carved corbel here, a decorative molding there—as if the building itself is breathing in and out with the night air.

The croquet lawn, still perfectly maintained, becomes a silver stage in full moonlight. Shadow-players seem to move across its surface—ladies with parasols, gentlemen in waistcoats—their forms suggested by shifting clouds across the moon, their stories written in patterns of light and dark on the dew-dampened grass.

Even the Club's famous clock tower plays its part in

this midnight performance. Moonlight catches the white faces of its four clock faces, making them glow like phantom moons themselves. The shadow of its hands moves with imperceptible slowness across these illuminated discs, marking time in a place where time itself seems to have stopped.

Inside, through windows that have watched over a century of American history, soft security lights create warm pools that only enhance the mystery. They catch on polished banisters, gleam off gilt-framed mirrors, and turn empty corridors into galleries of shadow and suggestion.

This is the hour when Jekyll Club is most itself—when the modern world recedes and the essence of what it was, what it remains, emerges from the interplay of moonlight and shadow. Here, after midnight, you can almost hear the rustle of silk dresses on grand staircases, almost smell the Cuban cigars on the veranda, almost see the flicker of gaslight in long-dark sconces.

The night air carries the salt smell of marsh and sea, while distant waves provide a gentle backbeat to the visual symphony of light and shadow. This is how the Club has stood for over a century—proud, elegant, slightly mysterious—its midnight face perhaps more true than its daylight one.

43

Light Through Tobacco Barns

In North Carolina's tobacco country, where weathered barns stand like ancient sentinels in fading fields, light becomes something sacred. Through gaps in aged oak boards, sunbeams pierce darkness like divine fingers, turning floating dust into constellations and drying tobacco leaves into stained glass.

Morning arrives in layers. First light sneaks through the highest cracks, creating golden bars that hang in empty air. As the sun climbs, these beams slide down weather-silvered walls, illuminating tier after tier of hanging tobacco, each leaf becoming translucent in its turn. The light reveals subtle gradients of color—from deep bronze to honey gold—as the leaves cure in warm darkness.

Inside these wooden cathedrals, the air itself seems to hold light differently. Dust motes dance in the beams, rising and falling like slow-motion fireflies, each particle catching fire for a moment before drifting back into shadow. The sweet, heavy scent of curing tobacco mingles with aged wood and morning air, creating an atmosphere that exists nowhere else on earth.

Through knotholes and warped boards, light paints ever-changing patterns on dirt floors that have supported generations of farmers' boots. These spots of brightness move with the sun's journey, marking time as they have since these barns first rose from red clay soil. Each beam tells a different story—some sharp and straight like sword cuts, others soft and diffused like brush strokes.

Mid-day brings its own magic. When the sun rides highest, light fills the upper reaches of the barn with a golden haze that filters down through the hanging leaves. Looking up through the tiers becomes like gazing through layers of amber, each level of tobacco creating its own shade of translucence, its own quality of glow.

The leaves themselves become performers in this daily light show. As they dry, they curl and twist, creating new openings for light to find its way through. Each movement, each curling edge, changes how sunlight breaks and bends. The result is an ever-shifting canvas of shadow and illumination, never the same from one moment to the next.

Late afternoon light arrives at a slant, turning the barn's western wall into a study in contrast. Here, the gaps between boards create bright lines that slice through dim air like golden knife cuts. These beams catch the edges of drying leaves, setting them aflame with rim lighting that transforms humble tobacco into botanical jewelry.

But it's not just about beauty—this interplay of light and shadow serves a practical purpose. Farmers read the quality of their cure in how light plays through the leaves, judging color and texture in bars of sunlight that have measured tobacco seasons longer than any living memory.

As evening approaches, the light show reaches its crescendo. Final rays of sun, heavy and gold as honey, create one last display before surrendering to dusk. These last beams seem to linger, as if reluctant to leave, turning dust motes into falling stars and lending tobacco leaves one final holy glow before night claims the barn.

In an age of climate-controlled curing barns and mechanical harvesting, these old light shows grow rarer with each passing season. Yet in the remaining wooden barns, where sunlight still finds its way through warped boards and weathered walls, magic still happens. Here, in these aging temples of agriculture, light still transforms humble leaves into art, still tells stories of soil and sun, still turns simple farming into something approaching grace.

44

The Light in Her Eyes

Miss Sarah Beth Morgan has lived in that corner house on Savannah's Lafayette Square since before I was born, and folks say the light in her eyes has never dimmed, even now in her ninety-third year. It's a particular kind of Southern light—part mischief, part steel magnolia, part ancient wisdom that comes from watching the world turn through nearly a century of Georgia summers.

When she sits in her front parlor, where afternoon sun filters through wavy antebellum glass, that light in her eyes seems to dance with the dust motes. She'll tell you stories of debutante balls from 1949, of secret gardens and midnight adventures, her eyes sparkling like river water catching sunrise. Each tale comes with a gleam that suggests there's always more to the story than what she's telling.

"The trick," she'll say, patting your hand with fingers thin as bird bones but strong as Spanish moss, "is to keep the light burning inside no matter what shadows life throws your way." And you believe her, because that's exactly what she's done through war and peace, through love and loss, through all the changes that have swept through Savannah like tide through marsh grass.

That light flashes quicksilver-bright when she laughs, which is often. It turns warm as honey when she speaks of her late Henry, grows sharp as cut crystal when she discusses politics, softens like twilight when neighborhood children bring her flowers from their mothers' gardens. It's a light that transforms her face from merely elderly to timelessly beautiful, as if illuminated from within by some eternal flame.

On her porch, where she holds court most evenings, that light in her eyes mingles with sunset's glow. Young couples stop to pay respects, drawn by the radiance of her smile as much as by Southern manners. She knows all their names, their stories, their dreams. The light brightens when she sees young love blooming, knowing some things never change in Savannah, no matter how many years pass.

Even in moments of sadness—remembering friends long gone, speaking of changes that haven't been for the better—the light never fully dims. It shifts and changes like sunshine through oak leaves, but it remains. "Darkness may visit," she'll tell you, smoothing her dress with practiced grace, "but I never invite it to stay for tea."

That light burns brightest when she speaks of hope, of tomorrow, of the future she sees in the eyes of children playing in her beloved square. It's a light that believes in possibility, in the power of grace under pressure, in the strength of Southern women who wear steel in their souls and sunshine in their smiles.

Some say it's just the natural optimism of a woman who's lived a blessed life. Others swear it's something more—a special kind of luminescence passed down through generations of Georgia women who learned to light their own way through dark times. Whatever its source, that light in Miss Sarah Beth's eyes has become as much a part of Lafayette Square as the fountain or the iron gates.

As twilight settles over Savannah like a prayer shawl, that light in her eyes seems to gather strength, as if preparing to hold back the darkness for one more night. And you understand, sitting there on her porch while lightning bugs rise from her garden like stars coming home, that some lights never truly dim—they just get passed along, story by story, smile by smile, heart by heart, until they become part of the city's eternal glow.

45

The Resurrection Gardens

Birmingham, Alabama

Where railroad tracks once divided neighborhoods like mason jars on a pantry shelf, Miss Bea's flowers now bloom in defiance of history. The old steel mill's shadow still falls across this part of Birmingham, but these days it falls on dahlias instead of dust, on raised beds of collards instead of coal slag, on hope growing in neat rows where despair once ruled.

It started with a single marigold pushing through a crack in the concrete. Miss Bea Washington, whose grandfather worked the furnaces until they went cold, saw that stubborn flower and recognized a fellow fighter. "If that little thing could bloom in all this ugly," she says, hands deep in composted soil, "then Lord knows we could do something with the rest of it."

That something became the Resurrection Gardens, a string of pocket parks and community gardens that now thread through Birmingham's industrial corridors like a green necklace. Where chain-link once rusted, grapevines now climb. Where broken bottles gathered, herb gardens now flourish. Where people once hurried past with eyes down, they now stop to admire Miss Bea's famous purple beans climbing up old mill pipes repurposed as trellises.

But these gardens grow more than vegetables. They grow community in soil enriched by history's hardships. White-haired men who once worked opposing shifts in the mill now work side by side, teaching young folks how to coax life from tired soil. Children whose grandparents couldn't share a water fountain now share watering cans, learning the democracy of growing things.

"Every seed planted is a prayer," Miss Bea tells the youngsters who come after school to tend their plots. "Every flower that blooms is an answer." She's transformed the old mill's loading dock into an outdoor classroom where science teachers bring students to learn about photosynthesis, and history teachers come to tell stories of the city's past while pointing toward its future.

The gardens have become bridges across Birmingham's old divides. The summer harvest suppers bring together folks from every corner of the city, all sharing dishes made from garden bounty. "Food grown together tastes better together," Miss Bea says, passing her famous pepper vinegar across tables that span generations and demographics.

On Sunday afternoons, the garden hosts what Miss Bea calls "Hymns and Horticulture," where gospel music mingles with the buzz of bees among the blossoms. The old mill's brick walls, once witnesses to division, now reflect back voices raised in harmony while hands of all shades work together in the soil.

Each season brings its own miracles. Spring sees children planting their first seeds, wide-eyed with possibility. Summer brings teenagers learning responsibility through tending their plots. Fall harvests become lessons in abundance and sharing. Even winter has its glory, as cold frames protect tender greens and prove that growth continues even when we can't see it.

The gardens have become more than just places to grow food—they're incubators of hope, proving grounds for possibility, and living lessons in how beauty can rise from ashes. Every bloom that opens, every vegetable that ripens, and every new friendship that forms across old boundaries stand as testament to the transformative power of working together in hope.

"We're growing more than gardens here," Miss Bea says, watching the sunset paint the old mill walls in colors that match her zinnias. "We're growing proof that anything can be resurrected if you add enough love, faith, and good old-fashioned stubborn hope."

And so, the gardens continue to spread, one plot at a time, healing old wounds with new growth, proving that even the hardest ground can yield to persistent tending, that the deepest divisions can be bridged by shared purpose, that resurrection isn't just a miracle—it's something we can grow together, one seed at a time.

46

The Porch Prophet

Richmond, Virginia

Miss Eugenia Fontaine's Victorian porch in Richmond's Fan District has been dispensing wisdom longer than most of its seekers have been alive. With its gingerbread trim casting lace-like shadows across heart pine floors and its ceiling painted the traditional paint blue, this porch has become an unofficial sanctuary where troubled souls find their way to healing, one rocking chair conversation at a time.

"The porch knows who needs it," Miss Eugenia says, her silver hair caught in an elegant chignon, her aging hands steady as she pours sweet tea into depression-glass tumblers. "I just provide the chairs and the listening." But anyone who's found their way to these worn floorboards knows it's more than that. Much more.

Corporate lawyers in tailored suits sit beside tattoo artists on their breaks. Debutantes share space with delivery drivers. Medical students from VCU find themselves pouring out their doubts beside retired janitors sharing their wisdom. Here, under the slow spin of ceiling fans, Richmond's carefully maintained social walls dissolve like sugar in summer tea.

Miss Eugenia holds court from her great-grandmother's rocker, its arms polished smooth by generations of hands seeking comfort. "Everyone's carrying something," she says. "Sometimes all they need is a safe place to set it down for a spell." Her porch has become that place—neutral ground in a city still healing from old wounds, still building bridges across ancient divides.

The regulars call her the Porch Prophet, though never to her face. They say she has a way of seeing straight to the heart of any trouble, of finding hope in the darkest stories. "She doesn't tell you what to do," says James Mitchell, a banker who first climbed these steps in despair and now stops by weekly to "maintain his spiritual account," as he puts it. "She helps you find your own answers, hiding there in plain sight like fireflies at dusk."

Young mothers bring colicky babies, finding peace in the porch's gentle rhythm. Teenagers slouch up the steps in rebellion but leave standing straighter, carrying new understanding of themselves and their parents. Even the mayor has been known to stop by, though Miss Eugenia treats him with the same gentle directness she offers everyone.

"The secret," she confides, adjusting a fern hanging in its

Victorian bracket, "is that most people already know what they need to do. They just need someone to listen while they find their way to knowing it." Her porch provides that space—a pause between thought and action, a shelter between problem and solution.

The porch's ministry continues through all seasons. Winter afternoons find visitors wrapped in quilts Miss Eugenia keeps in an old cedar chest, sharing coffee and confidences. Spring brings couples working through new love's uncertainties. Summer evenings overflow with neighbors seeking wisdom and breeze. Fall paints everything in golden light that seems to make truth easier to speak and harder to avoid.

Stories flow here like the James River through Richmond's heart—stories of loss and triumph, of fear and courage, of failures redeemed and success shared. Miss Eugenia listens to them all, offering what each soul needs: sometimes just silence, sometimes a pointed question, sometimes a piece of family wisdom passed down through generations of strong Virginia women who knew how to help hearts heal.

"Every porch is a bridge," Miss Eugenia says, watching lightning bugs rise from her carefully tended gardens. "Between inside and outside, between what is and what could be, between who we are and who we might become." Her porch has become more than that—it's become a landing place for troubled spirits, a launching pad for renewed hope, a sanctuary where Richmond's past and future meet to find their way forward together.

And so the porch prophet continues her gentle ministry, one conversation at a time, proving that sometimes the most powerful pulpit is a rocking chair, and the most profound sermon is simply learning to listen with love.

47

Hands That Build Dreams

Louisville, Kentucky

In a converted bourbon warehouse on Louisville's west side, where oak barrels once aged Kentucky's finest spirits, Marcus Thompson teaches young hands to coax beauty from wood. The sweet scent of fresh-cut cherry mingles with the lingering whispers of bourbon that still seep from the old walls, creating an atmosphere that speaks of both heritage and hope.

"Every piece of wood has a story," Marcus tells his students, mostly teenagers who've found their way here through court programs or school counselors. His own calloused hands move across a plank of reclaimed oak, reading its grain like Braille. "Just like every person has a story. Our job is to find the beauty in both."

The workshop, which he calls "Second Growth," fills what was once the barrel-aging floor. Where neat rows of bourbon barrels once rested, workbenches now stand in orderly formation. Each station is equipped with tools that Marcus has collected over decades—many donated by retiring craftsmen who believe in his mission of transformation through craftsmanship.

"See these knots?" he asks a young man whose own life has more than a few rough spots. "They're not flaws. They're character marks. The real art is working with them, not against them." The boy's hands, more used to making fists than furniture, slowly trace the wood's natural patterns, beginning to understand.

Marcus learned his craft from his father, who learned it from his father before him. But he's teaching more than woodworking here. Each project becomes a lesson in patience, in problem-solving, and in the dignity of work well done. "You can't rush wood," he tells them. "And you can't rush healing either."

The projects start simple—cutting boards, birdhouses, small boxes. But as skills grow, so do ambitions. Students graduate to chairs, tables, and even fine cabinets. Each piece they complete becomes tangible proof of their own capability, their own worth. "First time I finished a table," one young woman shares, "was the first time I felt like I could finish anything."

Local furniture stores now display their work proudly, with proceeds going back into the program. Restaurants commission tables made from reclaimed bourbon barrel staves. Interior designers seek out their unique pieces that tell stories of both wood and maker. But the real transformation happens at the workbench, where troubled youth find purpose in the patient shaping of raw wood into useful beauty.

"Wood teaches truth," Marcus says, helping a student through a difficult dovetail joint. "You can't lie to wood. It knows if you're rushing, if you're angry, or if you're not paying attention. It'll show every mistake. But it'll also show every moment of care, every bit of patience, and every ounce of love you put into it."

The workshop runs on more than just electricity. It runs on second chances, on belief in possibility, and on the transformative power of creating something beautiful with your own hands. Former students, now employed craftsmen themselves, return to mentor new arrivals. The cycle of healing continues, shaped like wood grain, one ring at a time.

As evening light filters through the warehouse's high windows, catching dust motes like floating gold, Marcus watches his students clean their workbenches and cover their projects. Some linger, reluctant to leave this space where they've found purpose and pride. "Tomorrow," he promises them. "The wood will be waiting."

And so, in this sacred space where bourbon once aged, young lives now age toward wisdom, shaped by caring hands and the patient teaching of wood. Each piece they create becomes more than furniture—it becomes proof that beauty can rise from rough beginnings, that careful hands can shape more than wood, and that dreams can be built one dovetail joint at a time.

48

The Sunday Singing Tree

Natchez, Mississippi

On a bluff high above the Mississippi River, where the setting sun paints the water in shades of glory, stands an oak tree older than the nation itself. Its branches, spread wide as God's own arms, have sheltered generations of song. This is Natchez's Sunday Singing Tree, where voices have risen in praise through war and peace, feast and famine, bondage, and freedom.

Every Sunday, just as the afternoon light turns honey-golden, people begin to gather. They come without formal invitation or announcement, drawn by tradition deeper than memory. Church ladies in their finest hats arrive bearing casserole dishes. Children in Sunday best chase each other through patches of clover. Young couples spread quilts in the dappled shade. The homeless man from downtown takes his place of honor near the trunk, his voice pure as spring water when he sings the old hymns.

"The tree remembers all the songs," says Mother Beatrice

Johnson, ninety-three years young, her voice still as strong as polished mahogany. "Every note ever sung here lives in those leaves." She's been coming to these gatherings since she was carried in her own mother's arms, and she's seen how the tree has served as more than just shelter from sun and rain.

During the Civil Rights era, when other gathering places were fractured by fear and hatred, the Singing Tree remained neutral ground. "Somehow," Mother Beatrice recalls, "standing under these branches, folks remembered they all knew the same hymns, all needed the same grace." Black and white voices found harmony here when they couldn't find it anywhere else.

The singing starts soft, usually with someone humming "Amazing Grace" or "Wade in the Water." Others join in, voices weaving together like Spanish moss in the breeze. There's no choir director, no piano, and no order of service. Just souls joining in song as the spirit moves them. The tree itself seems to participate, its leaves providing percussion in the river wind.

Young Darius Williams, home from college where he studies classical voice, stands near his great-grandmother, Mother Beatrice. His trained tenor soars above the crowd in "His Eye Is on the Sparrow," while she harmonizes below, their voices bridging generations. Children learn the old songs by osmosis, absorbing them like the tree absorbs sunlight, adding their clear, high voices to the chorus.

Between songs, covered dishes are opened, recipes exchanged, and stories shared. Miss Emma's chocolate pie disappears first, as it has for forty years. Brother Thomas's barbecue draws appreciative murmurs. The feast is informal, paper plates balanced on knees, everyone welcome to share, no one going hungry.

The tree has witnessed countless prayers, celebrations, and mournings. Babies who were once dedicated under its branches now bring their own children. Couples who first held hands in its shade return to renew their vows. When the levee threatened to break in the flood of '11, people gathered here to pray. When young soldiers shipped out to distant wars, the tree heard their mothers' prayers.

As sunset approaches, the singing takes on a deeper resonance. "Swing Low, Sweet Chariot" rolls down the bluff toward the river, where cargo ships sound their horns in response. The harmonies grow richer, voices blending like tributaries flowing into the mighty Mississippi below.

Sometimes, in the deepening twilight, Mother Beatrice will tell the young ones about the days when slaves gathered here in secret to sing their sorrows and their hopes. "This tree," she'll say, "has heard every kind of hallelujah there is." The children listen, wide-eyed, feeling the weight of history in every leaf above them.

As stars begin to appear, the gathering slowly disperses, but the songs linger in the air like incense. The old oak stands sentinel over the bluff, its branches still humming with centuries of hymns, its roots deep in Mississippi soil, its crown reaching toward heaven—a living testament to the power of song to heal, to unite, to lift spirits higher than any trouble can reach.

The Sunday Singing Tree remains, growing stronger with each passing season, each raised voice, each shared meal, and each moment of grace. It stands as proof that some traditions don't need walls or roofs, just open hearts and lifted voices, joining together under God's own cathedral of leaves.

49

Kitchen of Second Chances

New Orleans, Louisiana

Behind the faded grandeur of a Creole townhouse in the French Quarter, where street jazz mingles with the scent of simmering roux, Madame Marie's Kitchen of Second Chances serves up hope alongside its award-winning gumbo. Here, where the tiles are worn smooth by generations of hurrying feet, recovering addicts learn to rebuild their lives one recipe at a time.

"In New Orleans, we don't just cook food—we cook redemption," Madame Marie says, her silver dreadlocks wrapped elegantly in a purple silk scarf. Her own journey from addiction to restoration began in this very kitchen thirty years ago. Now she stands like a beacon, showing others the way back to dignity through the precise art of Creole cuisine.

The kitchen staff arrives before dawn—former dealers learning to measure ingredients instead of drugs, fallen bankers rediscovering self-worth in perfectly chopped trinity, and musicians who lost their way finding new rhythms in the percussion of knife on cutting board. Each one carries a story as complex as Madame Marie's secret spice blend, each one learning to taste hope again.

"First thing we learn here," says Marcus, a former jazz trumpeter now sous chef, "is that every ingredient matters. Just like every person matters. You can't make proper gumbo without all the parts working together." His hands, once shaky from withdrawal, now move with a surgeon's precision as he demonstrates the proper way to peel shrimp.

The restaurant operates on what Madame Marie calls "Trinity Time"—named for the holy trinity of Creole cooking: onions, celery, and bell peppers. "Everything happens when it's supposed to happen," she tells new arrivals. "You can't rush a roux any more than you can rush healing." The kitchen's pace teaches patience, precision, and the slow art of becoming.

Every station in the kitchen represents a step in recovery. New arrivals start at prep, learning to show up on time, to take direction, and to be reliable. As they prove themselves, they move up—to salads, to sauces, to the sacred responsibility of the roux. Each promotion comes with new challenges and new rewards, mirroring the journey from addiction to independence.

The menu changes daily, written on a weathered chalkboard in Madame Marie's elegant script. But certain dishes remain constant: hope served in a bowl of gumbo, dignity plated with red beans and rice, and pride presented in perfectly formed beignets. Every dish carries the essence of its maker's journey toward healing.

Local suppliers, many of them graduates of the program, arrive through the back door with fresh seafood, produce, and stories of their own continued recovery. Success breeds success here, creating a network of support as intricate as the flavor layers in Madame Marie's court bouillon.

The dining room itself serves as a testament to transformation. Crystal chandeliers salvaged from hurricane debris cast rainbow light across tables made by program graduates. The walls display local art created in recovery programs. Even the ancient ceiling fans tell stories of restoration, each one lovingly rebuilt by hands learning to create rather than destroy.

"Food is memory," Madame Marie often says, stirring a pot of her grandmother's gumbo. "But it's also the future. Every meal we serve is a promise that tomorrow can taste better than yesterday." Her kitchen has become more than just a restaurant—it's become a sanctuary where broken spirits learn to sing again, where lost souls find their way home through the familiar rituals of Louisiana cooking.

As evening service begins and the dining room fills with locals and tourists alike, the kitchen moves with the practiced grace of a second line parade. Orders flow, plates emerge, and lives continue their slow transformation. Above it all, Madame Marie watches with eyes that see past present struggles to future possibilities, seasoning each moment with equal measures of tough love and tender mercy.

In this kitchen of second chances, where steam rises like incense and pots bubble like prayers, New Orleans continues its ancient tradition of turning pain into beauty, loss into gain, and simple ingredients into something sacred. Each meal served becomes proof that restoration is possible, that rock bottom can become solid ground, and that even the most broken lives can be made whole again—one recipe, one day, one second chance at a time.

50

The Bicycle Minister

Rural Arkansas

Through the mist-wrapped hollows of the Ozarks, where dirt roads wind like brown ribbons through ancient hills, Brother James pedals his way through his unusual parish. His bicycle, an old Schwinn loaded with everything from Bibles to basic groceries, has become as familiar a sight as deer at dawn or turkey tracks in spring mud.

"The Lord didn't say we needed a fancy building to do His work," Brother James says, adjusting the bungee cords that hold his mobile ministry together. At sixty-eight, his legs are as strong as hickory, and his spirit is stronger still. The saddlebags on his bike carry more than physical supplies—they carry hope to places where paved roads and easy answers don't reach.

He started this bicycle ministry twenty years ago, after the last small churches in these remote hollows closed their doors. "Folks still needed the Word," he remembers, "and more than that, they needed to know somebody cared enough to come find them." So, he traded his pulpit for pedals and his church pews for mountain paths and found his true calling in the spaces between spaces.

Every day begins before sunrise, as Brother James consults his hand-drawn maps and weather-worn notebook. He knows which elderly widow needs her medication picked up from the valley pharmacy, which young mother could use some extra diapers, and which old-timer might not have eaten a proper meal in days. His route is planned around need rather than convenience, prayer mixed with practical help.

"Jesus fed people before He preached to them," he says, pushing his bike up a particularly steep section of mountain road. "Hard to hear the Gospel over a hungry stomach." So, his ministry includes everything from delivering groceries to helping fix leaky roofs, from reading letters to the illiterate to simply sitting and listening to folks who haven't had a visitor in weeks.

The children of the hollows watch for him like they watch for the ice cream truck in town. He carries hard candy in his pocket and hope in his heart, sharing both freely. To them, he's part Santa Claus, part guardian angel, his bicycle bells announcing that someone from the outside world remembers they exist.

In summer heat or winter chill, through rain and occasional snow, Brother James keeps his appointments. He's delivered babies, sat with the dying, counseled the troubled, and celebrated life's victories, all from the seat of his bicycle. His congregation doesn't gather in any building—they're connected by winding dirt roads and the faithfulness of a man who believes ministry happens best in motion.

The locals take care of him in their own way. A fresh pie might appear on a fence post along his route. Someone might leave a bag of fresh vegetables from their garden. During deer season, he never lacks for meat. "The Lord provides," he says, "usually through the hands of the very people I'm supposed to be helping."

His bike has become more than transportation—it's become a symbol of persistence, of faith that moves beyond four walls of love that's willing to go the extra mile. The rack over the back wheel has held everything from Christmas presents to newborn goats, while the front basket has carried Bibles, blood pressure medications, and once, memorably, a wounded owl he delivered to a wildlife rehabilitator.

As afternoon shadows lengthen across the hills, Brother James makes his final stops of the day. He knows which porches will have a chair waiting for him, which homes need a prayer, and which souls need reminding that they're not forgotten. His ministry is measured not in souls saved but in lives touched, not in sermons preached but in miles pedaled in service.

"Every revolution of these wheels is a prayer," he says, starting down a hill as sunset paints the Ozarks in heaven's own colors. "Every mile is worship. Every visit is church." And so, he pedals on, this circuit rider for modern times, proving that sometimes the most powerful ministry doesn't need a steeple—just two wheels, an open heart, and the willingness to go where you're needed.

51

Seeds of Promise

Eastern Tennessee

Deep in the folds of Tennessee's Smoky Mountains, where morning mist clings to ancient ridges like remembered dreams, Sarah Mae Tillery tends to what might be the most precious bank vault in Appalachia. But instead of money, these safety deposit boxes hold seeds—thousands of them, each one carrying stories as rich as the soil they spring from.

The Heritage Seed Library, housed in a converted general store that's stood in Hampton Valley since 1902, looks more like a living museum than a seed bank. Mason jars line wooden shelves, their contents carefully labeled in flowing script: "Walking Stick Bean - Passed down by Walker family since 1889," "Aunt Bessie's German Pink Tomato," "Lightning Flash Corn - Survives drought, feeds hope."

"Every seed tells a story," Sarah Mae says, her silver hair caught up in a faded bandana as she sorts through this season's new arrivals. "And every story feeds somebody." Her own story started forty years ago, when she realized that old-time mountain varieties were disappearing faster than spring snow. She began collecting not just seeds, but the wisdom that went with them.

The library operates on a simple principle: take what you need, grow what you take, and return what you can. It's become more than just a seed exchange—it's become a living archive of mountain culture, a genetic trust fund ensuring that future generations will taste the same beans their great-grandparents grew and will know the same garden wisdom that sustained families through lean times.

Local children come after school to help sort and package seeds, learning the difference between pole beans and bush beans and understanding why some corn is called "sweet" and some "dent." They learn more than botany—they learn their own history, written in the DNA of plants their ancestors developed through generations of careful selection.

"See these beans?" Sarah Mae asks a wide-eyed girl, holding up a jar of mottled seeds the color of sunset. "Your great-grandmother brought these over the mountain in her apron pocket when she came here as a bride. Now they feed families all through this valley." The child reaches for the jar with reverent hands, suddenly understanding that she's part of something larger than herself.

The library serves more than just gardeners. It's become

a gathering place where old-timers share planting wisdom with newcomers, where struggling families find hope in paper packets of possibility, and where mountain traditions take root in fresh soil. On Saturday mornings, the front porch hosts what Sarah Mae calls "Seed and Story Swaps," where trading seeds becomes an excuse for trading life wisdom.

Through a partnership with local food banks, the library helps establish community gardens in food deserts, teaching people not just how to grow food but how to save seeds for next year's crop. "Knowledge that isn't shared withers like an unpicked bean," Sarah Mae says, demonstrating the proper way to shell leather britches beans to a young mother.

The seed library's influence spreads like wild grapevines through the mountains. Small satellite collections have sprouted in church basements and community centers across five counties. Each one becomes a hub of hope, a place where people remember that wealth isn't always measured in dollars, but sometimes in the seeds of tomorrow's dinner.

As climate changes and commercial seed varieties narrow, Sarah Mae's collection becomes more precious with each passing season. These hardy mountain varieties, developed through generations of trial and error, might hold keys to feeding future generations. Each seed carries not just genetic material, but the accumulated wisdom of centuries of mountain gardeners who knew how to coax abundance from tough soil and short seasons.

In the cool darkness of the seed room, where future gardens sleep in labeled jars, Sarah Mae continues her quiet work of preservation and possibility. She's teaching a new generation that some banks hold wealth that can't be measured in money—wealth that grows with each sharing, multiplies with each planting, and feeds both body and soul with each harvest.

"We're not just saving seeds," she says, watching evening light paint the mountains in shades of forever. "We're saving who we are, who we were, and who we might become." And so, the seeds sleep in their jars, each one carrying promise, each one waiting to prove that hope, properly planted and tended, grows into tomorrow's abundance.

52

The Memory Quilters

Coastal North Carolina

In a weathered white house overlooking Pamlico Sound, where salt breeze carries stories like scattered cotton, the Memory Quilters gather every Tuesday to stitch life's fragments into something beautiful. They call themselves the Pieced Together Sisters, though not all are related by blood—they're bound by something stronger: the need to make sense of loss through the ancient art of quilting.

It started after Hurricane Florence, when Miss Pearl Johnson found her grandmother's wedding dress tangled in a cypress tree. The dress was ruined, but she couldn't bear to throw it away. "Some things are too precious to lose," she says, running weathered fingers across a quilt square made from that same water-stained silk. "Sometimes you have to destroy something to save it."

Now the house fills each Tuesday with women bearing their own precious scraps: pieces of uniforms from soldiers

who didn't come home, baby clothes outgrown too quick-
ly, work shirts worn thin by years of honest labor. Each
piece carries a story, and as the women work, their voices
rise and fall like waves on the nearby shore, weaving tales
as intricate as their stitching.

"We're not just making quilts," says Ruby Mae Collins,
carefully positioning a piece of her father's fishing shirt
next to her mother's church dress. "We're stitching memories back together." Her latest work, "Storm Surge," com-
bines fragments from three generations of hurricane survival into a swirling pattern that somehow captures both
chaos and hope.

The quilters work with more than cloth. They piece
together grief and joy, loss and recovery, past and future.
Their stitches are like tiny prayers, holding together not
just fabric but the very fabric of their community. Each
finished quilt becomes more than just a blanket—it becomes a map of survival, a testament to resilience, a story
told in texture and color.

Young women come too, bringing pieces of their own
stories to add to the larger pattern. They learn more than
quilting here—they learn how to weather life's storms,
how to make beauty from wreckage, how to stitch hope
into tomorrow. The older women's hands guide them
through more than just proper seam allowances; they
guide them through grief, through change, through rebuilding.

The house itself has become part of the story. Hurricane-scarred but standing proud, it offers shelter to more than just quilters. People bring their broken things here—not just fabric, but broken hearts, broken dreams, broken faith. Somehow, in the gentle rhythm of needle and thread, healing begins. "Every stitch is a step forward," Miss Pearl says. "Every finished square is a victory."

Their quilts tell stories that words alone cannot capture: the way moonlight looks on flood water, the sound of wind taking away everything you own, the feeling of community coming together to rebuild. Blues and greys swirl into hurricane patterns, bright patches of hope peek through dark moments, and always, always, there are stitches holding everything together.

Some quilts go to families who've lost everything to storms. Others hang in the local museum, recording history in fabric and thread. Still others travel to disaster areas across the country, carrying comfort and connection from one survivor to another. Each one carries a piece of the coast's story, stitched with love and understanding by hands that know both loss and hope.

As evening approaches and the light turns golden across the sound, the women gather their work into bags made from old feed sacks. They leave different than they came—lighter somehow, stronger, more whole. Their quilts may never hang in fancy galleries, but they hang in homes where they're needed most, wrapping survivors in tangible proof that beauty can rise from chaos, that community can weather any storm, that love can be stitched into every broken place.

The house stands quiet in the gathering dusk, waiting for next Tuesday's gathering. Inside, squares of fabric lie ready for tomorrow's stories, threads wait to connect past to future, and always, there's room for one more person who needs to piece their life back together, one stitch at a time.

In this sacred space where memories meet hope, the Memory Quilters continue their gentle work of transformation, proving that sometimes the strongest rebuilding happens not with hammer and nail, but with needle and thread, with loving hands and understanding hearts, with stories shared and sorrows stitched into something beautiful enough to pass down to generations yet to come.

53

The Manatee Whisperer

The Florida Keys

In the gentle waters of a Florida Keys sanctuary, where morning light dapples the surface like scattered gold coins, Doctor Rosa Mendez doesn't so much work with manatees as she communes with them. Known locally as "The Manatee Whisperer," she's spent thirty years healing not just injured sea cows but also wounded souls through what she calls "manatee medicine."

"They're living zen masters," Rosa says, her silver-streaked hair caught up in a weather-beaten Key West Rescue cap as she checks on her latest patient, a young male injured by a boat propeller. "They teach us how to move through life's troubles with grace, how to heal without bitterness, and how to trust after being hurt."

The sanctuary, tucked into a quiet canal where royal palms reflect in turquoise water, has become more than just a rehabilitation center for injured manatees. It's become a place of healing for people too. Veterans with

PTSD find peace in the slow, gentle presence of these massive creatures. Children with autism connect in ways that surprise their therapists. Troubled teens learn patience and compassion while helping with rehabilitation.

"Watch," Rosa whispers to a group of at-risk youth as a massive female manatee named Grace approaches the dock. "She was hurt badly by humans, but she still chooses to trust." The teenagers, usually tough as mangrove roots, soften visibly as Grace rolls over for a belly rub, her scars telling stories of survival that these streetwise kids understand all too well.

The sanctuary operates on what Rosa calls "manatee time"—slow, deliberate, peaceful. There's no rushing here, no hurrying healing. Injured manatees stay until they're ready to return to the wild, and troubled humans stay until they find their own path to peace. "The manatees know," Rosa says. "They always know who needs them most."

Local fishermen bring injured manatees here, but they also bring their troubles. Rosa has seen weather-beaten men cry while helping tend to wounded calves, finding their own healing in the act of helping these gentle giants. She's watched hardened hearts soften in the presence of mothers nursing their babies and witnessed miracles of transformation that have nothing to do with veterinary medicine and everything to do with soul medicine.

The sanctuary's volunteer program has a waiting list years long. People come from all over to help, but Rosa chooses her volunteers carefully. "The manatees choose too," she says. "They know who's ready to learn what they have to teach." Those chosen find themselves part of something larger than themselves—a circle of healing that encompasses both species.

Each morning begins with what Rosa calls "manatee meditation." Volunteers sit quietly by the water, watching these peaceful creatures glide through early light. "They teach us to slow down, to breathe, to be present," she explains. "In a world that moves too fast, they show us the power of moving slowly, deliberately, with purpose."

The sanctuary's work extends beyond its quiet waters. Rosa and her team work tirelessly to educate boaters about manatee safety, to protect the seagrass beds these gentle creatures depend on, and to ensure that future generations will know the peace of sharing space with these living embodiments of tranquility.

As sunset paints the water in shades of rose and gold, Rosa makes her final rounds. She knows each manatee by name, knows their stories, their personalities, and their healing journeys. They surface as she passes, their whiskered faces wise as ancient monks, their eyes holding secrets of deep water and deeper peace.

"They remind us," she says, watching a mother and calf glide past in the golden light, "that gentleness is not weakness, that moving slowly is not the same as standing still, that healing happens in its own time." And so, the sanctuary continues its quiet work, offering peace to all who seek it, proving that sometimes the most profound healing comes not from medicine, but from moments of connection with creatures who have mastered the art of being simply, perfectly themselves.

In these sacred waters, where injured manatees find healing and troubled humans find hope, Rosa continues her gentle ministry of interspecies healing, showing that sometimes the best medicine doesn't come in pills or prescriptions but in the peaceful presence of thousand-pound angels with flippers and whiskers.

54

The Mountain Music Maker

Blue Ridge, Georgia

In a sunlit workshop tucked into the misty folds of the Blue Ridge Mountains, William "Uncle Bill" McCreary's hands move across maple and spruce with the same reverence his grandfather's did. Here, where wood shavings curl like memories on the floor and the scent of fresh-cut cedar mingles with history, he crafts more than just dulcimers—he builds bridges between past and future.

"Every instrument has a soul waiting to be freed," Uncle Bill says, holding a half-finished dulcimer up to catch morning light through its sound holes. At seventy-eight, his hands are maps of a life spent coaxing music from wood, each scar and callus marking decades of dedication to an art form older than the mountains themselves.

But it's not just instruments he's preserving. Three days a week, his workshop transforms into a classroom where troubled youth from across North Georgia come to learn more than woodworking. They learn patience through careful sanding, discipline through precise measurements, and pride through creating something beautiful with their own hands.

"Music and woodworking speak the same language," he tells a young man carefully shaping a dulcimer's neck. "Both require listening deeper than just with your ears." The boy, sent here by a juvenile court judge as an alternative to detention, nods slowly, understanding dawning in his eyes as his hands learn the wisdom of wood.

The walls of Uncle Bill's workshop tell stories of their own. Photographs of past students and their creations hang alongside vintage instruments. Each image captures a moment of transformation—the proud smile of a first-time builder holding their completed dulcimer, the concentrated focus of young hands learning ancient skills, the joy of creating something that sings.

"These kids come here thinking they're going to learn about woodworking," says Sarah Beth, a local teacher who helps coordinate the program. "They leave having learned about themselves." The process of creating an instrument from raw wood becomes a metaphor for their own transformation—rough edges smoothed by patience, discord turned to harmony, beauty emerging from seeming chaos.

Every Wednesday evening, the workshop hosts what Uncle Bill calls "picking and learning" sessions. Students past and present gather to play the instruments they've built, their music mixing with the sound of whip-poor-wills and evening wind in the pines. Old-timers share tunes passed down through generations, while young hands learn to coax ancient melodies from strings, they stretched themselves.

The impact reaches beyond the workshop walls. Former students have gone on to start their own businesses, become teachers themselves, and found ways to give back to their communities. "When you learn to create beauty," Uncle Bill says, "you learn to see it everywhere." Some return years later, bringing their own children to learn the ways of wood and music.

Local timber companies donate special cuts of wood—maple, cherry, and spruce—knowing these materials will become instruments that keep mountain music alive. Hardware stores contribute tools, music shops provide strings and tuners, and the community rallies around this unique program that builds both instruments and character.

As afternoon sun slants through dusty workshop windows, Uncle Bill guides a young girl's hands as she fits a bridge to her first dulcimer. Her face glows with concentration, all her usual teenage defenses forgotten in the focus of creation. "That's it," he encourages, "let the wood tell you what it needs."

The workshop fills with the gentle sounds of creation—sandpaper whisking across wood, careful tapping of bridges being fitted, and soft humming as students work. These are the sounds of healing, of growth, of tradition being passed from one generation to the next through hands that learn to create rather than destroy.

In this sacred space where sawdust glitters like gold in sunbeams and ancient tunes float through evening air, Uncle Bill continues his quiet ministry of transformation. Each instrument that leaves his workshop carries more than just the potential for music—it carries the promise that beauty can be created by anyone willing to learn its language, that harmony can be found in the most unexpected places, and that some of life's deepest lessons can be taught by wood and strings and patient hands that know how to listen.

55

The Letter Lady

Abbeville, South Carolina

Behind the worn wooden counter of Abbeville's century-old post office, Miss Geneva Washington has been more than just a postmaster for forty-three years. She's become the town's unofficial scribe, confidante, and keeper of stories, helping those who can't read or write stay connected with loved ones far away.

"Words are bridges," Geneva says, her silver-framed glasses catching morning light as she helps Mr. Thompson, ninety-two and nearly blind, compose another letter to his granddaughter in California. "Sometimes they're the only way across the distances that life puts between people."

Her official hours are nine to five, but Geneva arrives early each morning to help those who need their letters read or written before work. She stays late too, knowing some folks can only come after their shifts end. Her small office, with its decades-old desk and creaking wooden chair, has become a sanctuary where dignity and privacy are as sacred as sealed envelopes.

"Miss Geneva gave my mama's words wings," says Darlene Cooper, whose mother never learned to write but kept her family together through twenty years of Geneva's letter-writing help. "Every week, she'd tell Miss Geneva what to say, and those letters kept us connected even when life scattered us across the country."

The walls of her office tell stories of their own—photographs of military reunions made possible by letters she helped write, wedding invitations for couples who met through correspondence she facilitated, and graduation announcements for students she encouraged through written words. Each image represents connections maintained, bridges built, and hope sustained through the power of written words.

Geneva's ministry of words extends beyond just letter writing. She helps fill out job applications, explains official documents, and translates government forms into language people can understand. During tax season, her lunch hours become impromptu assistance sessions. "Understanding is a basic human right," she says, helping a young mother decipher her first mortgage application.

But it's the letters that remain her true calling. She has an uncanny ability to capture each person's unique voice, to put their heart on paper in a way that feels authentic and personal. "Everyone has their own way of speaking love," she explains, carefully writing out a grandmother's birthday wishes to a grandchild she's never met. "My job is just to help that love find its way to paper."

The stories flow through her office like water: migrant workers sending money and love back home, children writing to incarcerated parents, and elderly folks maintaining connections with family scattered across the country. Geneva handles each story with gentle respect, each letter with careful attention, and each person with unwavering dignity.

Her own story is written in the thousands of letters she's helped create over four decades. Some folks call her the "Angel of the Post Office," but she brushes such praise aside. "I'm just doing what needs doing," she says, though the drawers full of thank-you cards and wedding invitations suggest her impact runs deeper than she'll admit.

As email and text messages reshape communication, Geneva's ministry becomes even more precious. She bridges not just literacy gaps but generational ones, helping grandparents connect with grandchildren who live in a digital world and teaching young folks the power of a handwritten letter.

"In a world of instant messages," she says, watching afternoon light paint shadows across her desk, "there's still something holy about sitting down and really thinking about what you want to say to someone you love." And so, she continues her quiet work, helping love find its way to paper, helping words build bridges across all the distances that life creates.

In her gentle presence, surrounded by the tools of her calling—pens, papers, envelopes, stamps—Geneva continues to prove that sometimes the most powerful ministry isn't preaching or teaching, but simply helping people's hearts find their way to paper, one letter at a time.

56

The Bicycle Angel

Itta Bena, Mississippi

Miss Thelma Lee's backyard in Itta Bena looks like a bicycle hospital. Rusty frames hang from pecan tree branches, wheels lean against her weathered fence like giant metal flowers, and handlebars sprout from over-turned milk crates. But to the children of this small Delta town, it's nothing less than a miracle factory.

For thirty-two years, Miss Thelma has been collecting, fixing, and giving away bicycles to any child who needs one. "Every kid deserves wings," she says, her work-worn hands steady as she adjusts a chain on a small pink bike. At seventy-four, she can still true a wheel better than most bike shop mechanics, a skill she learned from her father, who ran the town's hardware store decades ago.

Her ministry began with one broken bicycle and a neighbor's child who needed a way to get to school. "That first repair job was mostly baling wire and prayer," she laughs, remembering. "But seeing that child ride away like he owned the world—well, that's when I knew what the Lord wanted me to do with my retirement."

Word spread through the Delta's small towns like wind through cotton fields. Soon, people started leaving broken bicycles on her porch at night, like offerings to a mechanical saint. Police departments donate unclaimed bikes. Church groups organize collection drives. But it's the repairs themselves that Miss Thelma sees as her real mission.

"It's not just about fixing bikes," she explains, showing a young boy how to oil a rusty chain. "It's about fixing hope." She requires every child who receives a bike to learn basic maintenance. Her Saturday morning repair clinics have become legendary, with children sprawled across her yard learning the gospel of self-reliance through basic mechanics.

The lessons go beyond bikes. "When something's broken," she tells her young apprentices, "You've got three choices. You can throw it away, you can pay somebody else to fix it, or you can learn to fix it yourself. Life's the same way." Her quiet wisdom, delivered between demonstrations of patch kits and brake adjustments, has helped guide more than one struggling child toward a better path.

Local teachers note that children who've received Miss Thelma's bikes show improved attendance and attitudes. "There's something about having your own transportation," says Mrs. Johnson from the elementary school, "that makes a child stand taller." Some former recipients, now grown with children of their own, bring their kids' bikes to Miss Thelma for repairs, completing a circle of community care.

Her yard has become more than just a repair shop—it's become a gathering place where children learn that broken things don't have to stay broken, that every problem has a solution if you're willing to learn, and that sometimes the best way to help yourself is to help others. Teenagers who started as recipients now volunteer, learning mechanical skills that some have turned into careers.

On hot Delta afternoons, Miss Thelma serves cold lemonade and life lessons from her porch, watching children test their newly repaired bikes in wobbly circles around her yard. "Freedom ain't free," she'll tell them, "But sometimes it just costs a little elbow grease and knowing how to use a wrench."

She keeps a photo album of every child with their first bike, pages and pages of pure joy captured in snapshots. "These aren't just pictures of bikes," she says, turning pages filled with three decades of smiling faces. "These are pictures of possibilities."

As evening approaches and the last young mechanics head home, Miss Thelma surveys her yard of metal possibilities. Tomorrow will bring more broken bikes, more children needing wings, and more opportunities to teach the gospel of self-reliance and hope through the simple act of fixing what's broken.

In this small Delta town, where opportunities sometimes seem as rare as rain in August, Miss Thelma continues her quiet revolution of restoration, proving that
sometimes the most powerful way to lift a community is
two wheels at a time.

57

The Story Keeper

Beaufort, South Carolina

I n a pale-yellow house on Bay Street, where ceiling fans spin lazy circles above floor-to-ceiling bookshelves, Miss Adelaide Caldwell maintains what she calls her "Living Library of Southern Souls." It's not a conventional library—you won't find card catalogs or late fees here. Instead, for forty-seven years, she's been collecting and preserving the oral histories of everyday people whose stories might otherwise fade like old photographs.

"Everyone has a story worth saving," Adelaide says, adjusting her tortoiseshell glasses as she sets up her ancient tape recorder. At eighty-one, her mind remains sharp as a sweetgrass needle, cataloging thousands of stories from shrimpers and sharecroppers, debutantes and domestic workers, each one carefully preserved in both digital files and her legendary memory.

The front parlor, with its worn leather chairs and perpetually steeping tea, has become a confessional of sorts.

People come here to share their memories—of civil rights struggles and church suppers, of hurricane survival and family traditions, of small triumphs and large heartbreaks. Adelaide records them all, her gentle questions drawing out details that might otherwise be lost to time.

"Miss Adelaide helped me find my grandmother's voice," says Marcus Washington, holding a CD recording of his grandmother's stories about growing up on a Sea Island in the 1920s. "After she passed, hearing her stories in her own words... it was like having her back for a little while."

Her collection defies traditional categorization. Stories of traditional sweetgrass basket weaving sit alongside accounts of modern shrimping practices. Tales of debutante balls share shelf space with memories of civil rights sit-ins. Each recording carries a piece of Beaufort's soul, preserved in the actual voices of those who lived it.

But Adelaide does more than just collect stories—she connects them. She'll introduce young craftspeople to elderly artisans, link newcomers with old-timers, help families find their own lost histories. "Stories are like Spanish moss," she says. "They all connect somewhere if you follow them long enough."

Every Thursday evening, she hosts what she calls "Story Circles" where people gather to share tales and memories. Young folks sit at the feet of elders, learning history not from books but from those who lived it. Sometimes the stories flow like tide water; sometimes they come hard as hurricane rain. Adelaide moderates with gentle skill, knowing when to prompt and when to let silence speak its own truth.

Her work has become increasingly urgent as older generations pass on. She's trained a group of young "Story Catchers" who help record and digitize memories, ensuring that this living history continues beyond her time. Local schools bring students to learn interviewing techniques, teaching them that every family's story adds to the larger narrative of the South.

The technology has changed over the years—from reel-to-reel tapes to digital recordings—but Adelaide's method remains the same. "People need to be heard," she says, "really heard, not just listened to." Her patience and genuine interest have drawn out stories that might never have been told otherwise.

As afternoon light slants through live oak leaves outside her windows, Adelaide reviews her latest recordings. Each one captures more than just words—they preserve accents, laughter, sighs, the very breath of history. Her cataloging system might puzzle professional librarians, but she can find any story in her collection within minutes.

"When we lose a story," she says, carefully labeling a new recording, "we lose a piece of ourselves. But when we save one, we save more than just memories—we save the wisdom that comes from living through something and making sense of it."

In this house full of voices from the past and present, Adelaide continues her gentle work of preservation, proving that sometimes the most valuable library isn't one that lends books, but one that lends ears to the stories that need telling, eyes to the histories that need seeing, and heart to the memories that need keeping.

For in these collected voices, preserved with love and shared with purpose, the soul of the South lives on, not just as history, but as living inspiration for generations to come.

58

The Angel of Apartment C

Nashville, Tennessee

In a modest apartment complex on the east side of Nashville, where tour buses never venture and rhinestones rarely shine, Miss Ruby Mae Jackson orchestrates small miracles from her ground-floor apartment. At ninety-two, she's become the unofficial grandmother to an ever-changing cast of aspiring musicians, struggling songwriters, and dreamers who've come to Music City with nothing but hope in their hearts and songs in their souls.

"Music feeds the spirit," Ruby Mae says, serving her famous cornbread to a young guitarist who hasn't eaten a proper meal in days. "But spirits need more than just songs to survive." Her tiny apartment, with its worn sofa and upright piano that's seen better days, has become a sanctuary for those whose Nashville dreams have hit hard times.

It started thirty years ago when she found a young man sleeping in his car in the apartment parking lot. He had a beat-up guitar, an empty stomach, and a dream of making it in country music. Ruby Mae fed him, let him shower in her apartment, and gave him a safe place to practice his songs. That singer now has gold records on his wall, but more importantly, he helped Ruby Mae realize her own calling.

Word spread through Nashville's underground music scene: if you're struggling, if you're hungry, if you need a grandmother's love and wisdom, find your way to Apartment C. Ruby Mae never turns anyone away. She's transformed her small apartment into what she calls her "Green Room Ministry," named after the waiting rooms where performers gather before shows.

"Some folks need a meal, some need advice, and some just need somebody to listen to their new song," she says, her fingers still strong enough to show a novice the proper way to form a G chord on her old piano. "But everybody needs somebody to believe in them, especially in this town."

Her walls tell stories of success and gratitude—signed photographs, platinum records, and handwritten lyrics framed with love. But Ruby Mae's proudest achievements aren't the ones who "made it big." They're the ones who found their way, whether that meant returning home with their dignity intact or discovering their true calling wasn't on stage but behind the scenes.

Every Sunday evening, she hosts what she calls "Family

Dinner and Song Circle." Musicians from all genres gather in her small living room, sharing food, songs, and stories. The only rule is that everyone must contribute something—a dish, a song, or a helping hand with cleanup. These gatherings have led to collaborations, friendships, and more than a few successful careers.

"Miss Ruby Mae taught me that Nashville isn't just about music," says Sarah Lynn Peters, now a successful songwriter. "It's about community. It's about lifting each other up when the lights are low and the crowds have gone home."

Her ministry extends beyond just musicians. She helps young artists navigate predatory contracts, connects struggling performers with honest managers, and isn't afraid to tell hard truths when needed. "Sometimes the kindest thing you can do is help somebody understand when it's time to find a new dream," she says, though she's quick to add, "But it's never time to stop dreaming altogether."

Local churches and food banks make sure her pantry stays stocked, knowing she'll distribute the goods where they're needed most. Music Row executives, many of whom found their own start on her worn sofa, quietly ensure her rent is always paid. But Ruby Mae's real currency is love, dispensed with wisdom earned through nine decades of watching dreams both soar and crash.

As evening settles over Nashville and the sound of practice rooms drifts through thin apartment walls, Ruby Mae sits in her favorite chair, listening to a young woman work through a new song. "Music City can be hard," she says, "but it doesn't have to be lonely."

In her small apartment, where country meets gospel meets blues meets hope, Ruby Mae continues her quiet ministry of encouragement, proving that sometimes the biggest dreams need the smallest stages to take flight and that every star that shines on Broadway first needed somebody who could see its light when it was still just a spark.

59

The Garden Angel

Charleston, South Carolina

Between stately South Battery mansions and modest Eastside homes, Sister Margaret Anne tends what locals call the "Miracle Gardens." At seventy-six, this former nun has transformed over thirty abandoned lots into flowering sanctuaries that feed both body and soul, but her real cultivation is hope, grown in the hearts of the city's most overlooked residents.

"Every garden needs three things," she says, her gardening clogs muddy and her white hair escaping from beneath a faded sunhat. "Good soil, tender care, and somebody who believes in what can grow." The same, she maintains, is true for people, and she cultivates both with equal devotion.

What began as a single vacant lot cleanup has blossomed into a network of urban gardens that dot Charleston's landscape like gems on velvet. Each garden serves multiple purposes: growing food for local families, providing job training for those seeking second chances, offering therapy for troubled youth, and creating peaceful spaces in concrete-bound neighborhoods.

"Sister Margaret didn't just plant flowers," says James Washington, who found his way to the gardens after prison. "She planted possibility." Now running his own landscaping business, James is one of countless individuals who discovered their path forward while learning to nurture growing things under Sister Margaret's patient guidance.

Her methods are as organic as her gardens. She matches elderly residents who can no longer maintain their yards with young people who need mentoring. Food bank clients become garden volunteers, earning fresh produce while learning valuable skills. Schoolchildren tend plots that supply their cafeterias, learning science and responsibility through hands-on experience.

"Gardens heal what doctors can't reach," she explains, helping a group of veterans tend their therapeutic flower beds. "Soil has its own medicine." Her partnership with local hospitals has created a groundbreaking horticultural therapy program, where patients find healing through working with plants.

The gardens themselves are masterpieces of creative repurposing. Old bathtubs become herb planters, broken concrete forms raised bed borders, and discarded pallets transform into vertical gardens. "Beauty doesn't need new things," Sister Margaret insists. "It just needs new eyes to see the potential in what's been thrown away."

Each garden develops its own personality and purpose. The Peace Garden, near a troubled housing project, has become neutral ground where rival groups find common purpose in growing things. The Memory Garden, filled with traditional healing plants, helps preserve Charleston's Gullah herbal wisdom. The Children's Garden teaches little ones that miracles can sprout from tiny seeds.

But perhaps her greatest gift is the way she helps people rediscover their own worth through nurturing life. Troubled teens learn patience watching seedlings emerge. Addicts in recovery find hope in the cycle of seasons. Elderly residents discover new purpose sharing their growing wisdom with younger generations.

As twilight settles over Charleston and the evening primrose opens to greet the moths, Sister Margaret makes her final rounds. She knows every plant, every volunteer, and every story of transformation. Her gardens have become more than just green spaces—they're incubators of hope, classrooms of second chances, and sanctuaries where life's hardest lessons can be learned through the gentle art of growing things.

"Every garden is an act of faith," she says, watching fireflies rise like prayers from the evening-scented flowers. "Faith in tomorrow, faith in the miracle of growth, faith in the possibility of beauty even in the hardest places."

And so, she continues her quiet ministry of cultivation, proving that sometimes the most powerful sermons aren't preached from pulpits but from potato patches, and that hope, like flowers, can bloom in the most unexpected places.

In these sacred spaces where soil meets soul, Sister Margaret tends not just gardens but possibilities, showing that with enough love, patience, and faith, anything can grow—even dreams that seemed as dead as winter ground.

60

The Legacy Keeper

Monroeville, Alabama

Miss Pearlie Mae Henderson sits on her wraparound porch in the heart of Monroeville, surrounded by what she calls her "Memory Boxes"—hundreds of carefully preserved photographs, letters, and artifacts that tell the story of small-town Southern life. At eighty-nine, she's become the unofficial historian of not just her town, but of the everyday moments that history books often forget.

"Everybody thinks history is just big moments and famous names," she says, carefully removing a 1940s church program from its acid-free sleeve. "But real history? That's in the church suppers, the Saturday morning haircuts, and the first day of school pictures. That's where you find the heart of who we are."

Her collection began sixty years ago with a single shoebox of photographs rescued from a neighbor's trash. "They were throwing away their grandma's whole life," she remembers, her voice still indignant. "Every picture is somebody's memory; every letter is somebody's heart speaking across time."

Now her home has become what locals call the "People's Museum." The formal dining room hosts carefully curated displays of everyday life—children's report cards from the one-room schoolhouse era, handwritten recipes that fed generations, and love letters from World War II soldiers to their sweethearts back home. Each item tells a story, and Miss Pearlie Mae knows them all.

But she does more than just preserve the past. Three times a week, she hosts "Memory Circles," where elderly residents share their stories while younger folks record them. High school students learn to conduct oral histories, capturing tales of everything from civil rights struggles to secret family recipes. "Every person who passes without sharing their story," she says, "takes a whole world of knowledge with them."

Her most powerful work happens when she connects people with their own lost histories. "Baby, come see this," she'll say, pulling out a photograph of someone's great-grandmother as a young woman. "This is where your smile comes from." She's helped dozens of families reconstruct their genealogies, fill in blank spaces in their family trees, and understand their place in the community's larger story.

The porch becomes a time machine on Sunday afternoons when she hosts "Story and Song" sessions. Old-timers share memories while children listen wide-eyed, learning their own history through tales of courage, perseverance, and occasional mischief. "These stories aren't just entertainment," she insists. "They're survival manuals for the heart."

Local teachers bring classes to learn history from artifacts they can hold in their hands—segregation-era "colored only" signs that spark difficult but necessary conversations, victory garden pamphlets from World War II, and handwritten poll tax receipts. "Some lessons," she says, "can only be learned by touching history."

Her work has taken on new urgency in the digital age. She's partnered with the local library to digitize her collection, ensuring these stories survive beyond her time. Young volunteers help scan photographs while she records the stories behind them, creating a multimedia archive of community memory.

"Every town needs a memory keeper," she says, carefully returning a 1923 graduation photograph to its protective sleeve. "Not just for the past's sake, but for the future. How can you know where you're going if you don't know where you've been?"

As evening settles over Monroeville and cicadas begin their twilight chorus, Miss Pearlie Mae rocks gently in her porch chair, surrounded by the collected memories of countless lives. Tomorrow will bring more stories to preserve, more connections to make, and more pieces of the past to protect for future generations.

In this sacred space where past meets present, Miss Pearlie Mae continues her gentle work of preservation, proving that sometimes the most valuable historical artifacts aren't in museums but in the carefully kept memories of those who understand that every life tells a story worth saving, every story holds a lesson worth learning, and every memory preserved is a gift to the future.

For in these collected moments, preserved with love and shared with purpose, the true history of the South lives on—not in textbooks or monuments, but in the everyday stories of ordinary people who lived extraordinary lives of courage, love, and resilience.

61

The Angel of Avenue B

Memphis, Tennessee

On a street where blues notes drift like smoke from corner clubs, Miss Ida Mae Thompson's front porch has become an unlikely classroom. Not the kind with desks and textbooks, but one where lost children find their way back to dreams through the power of words. At eighty-four, this former English teacher hasn't stopped changing lives—she's just moved her classroom from school to stoop.

"Poetry saved my life when I was thirteen," Miss Ida Mae says, adjusting her wire-rimmed glasses as she helps a teenage boy find rhythm in his rap lyrics. "Now I'm just passing that salvation forward." Her porch, with its mismatched chairs and overflowing bookshelves protected from rain by clear plastic, has become what the neighborhood kids call "The Word Shop."

It started fifteen years ago when she caught some boys writing graffiti on her fence. Instead of calling the police, she called them up to her porch and taught them about Langston Hughes. "If you're gonna write on walls," she told them, "At least make it poetry worth reading." Now those same boys, grown men with children of their own, send their kids to Miss Ida Mae to learn the power of their own voices.

Every afternoon, as the Memphis sun sinks toward the Mississippi, young people gather on her porch. Some come to learn how to turn their rap lyrics into sophisticated wordplay. Others come to find their voice through traditional poetry. All find an elder who believes that everyone has a poem inside them waiting to be heard.

"Miss Ida Mae taught me that Shakespeare and Tupac are asking the same questions," says Marcus Williams, now a published poet himself. "They're both trying to make sense of love and loss, life and death, hope and despair. She showed me how to bridge those worlds."

Her methods are as unconventional as her classroom. She'll help a young rapper find Shakespeare quotes to sample, teach grammar through freestyle battles, and show how ancient Greek meters can improve hip-hop flow. "Words don't care who uses them," she says. "They just want to dance."

The transformation happens slowly, but it happens. Young people who came clutching anger like a shield learn to wield words instead of weapons. Students who couldn't find their voice in traditional classrooms discover they've been poets all along. Gang members find a different kind of power in metaphor and rhyme.

The power of Miss Ida Mae's porch stretches far beyond poetry. Local teachers send her their troubled students—the ones labeled "difficult" or "unreachable." She sees past their defenses to the raw talent underneath. "Every angry word is just a love poem that lost its way," she tells them, and somehow, they begin to believe her.

Her library, built from yard sales and donations, spans from ancient classics to contemporary spoken word. She knows exactly which book to put in which hands—Maya Angelou for the quiet girl with fire in her eyes, Nikki Giovanni for the boy trying to understand his own anger, and Robert Frost for the teenager who feels lost in his own world.

"Poetry isn't just about pretty words," she tells a group of young men who've traded gang signs for sonnets. "It's about power. The power to name your pain, to claim your joy, to change your world one word at a time." Her graduates have gone on to start poetry clubs in schools, organize community open mics, and publish their own works. Some have even returned to college, discovering academic passion through creative expression.

Every Friday night, her porch hosts "Words and Wisdom"—an open mic session where young poets share their work alongside community elders sharing their stories. The mix of voices creates something magical—hip-hop verses flow into civil rights memories, slam poetry merges with gospel testimonies, and somewhere in between, understanding grows.

"Before Miss Ida Mae," says LaKeisha Johnson, now teaching creative writing at a local high school, "I thought poetry was just dead white men in dusty books. She showed me that poetry is alive in everything—in rap, in prayers, in playground rhymes, and in the way my grandmother tells stories. She taught me that my voice matters."

The porch has become a safe haven in more ways than one. Gang members declare it neutral territory. Police officers stop by to share their own poems. Parents know their children are safe here, wrapped in the protective power of words and wisdom. Even in Memphis's summer heat or winter chill, the porch remains a beacon of hope and possibility.

Miss Ida Mae keeps a journal of "porch moments"—small victories that mark big changes. The first time a shy student shares a poem. The day two rivals discover common ground in their verses. The moment when a young person realizes they have something valuable to say.

"Words can build bridges or walls," she tells her students. "The choice is yours." Her own choice has always been to build bridges—between generations, between cultures, and between who people are and who they dream of becoming.

As night falls over Memphis and porch lights flicker on like earthbound stars, Miss Ida Mae listens to her last student of the day work through a difficult verse. The street below echoes with blues music from nearby clubs, creating a backdrop for the young poet's words.

"That's it," she encourages, hearing the moment when rhythm and meaning finally merge. "Now you're not just speaking—you're singing." And in that moment, another voice finds its power, another story takes flight, and another life transforms through the magic of words set free.

In this sacred space where literature meets life, Miss Ida Mae continues her ministry of liberation through language, proving that sometimes the most powerful classroom has no walls, the most important lessons come with no grades, and the truest education happens when someone believes in the poet hiding inside every troubled heart.

For on this porch, where words dance between generations and hope rides on the wings of poetry, lives are being rewritten one verse at a time, proving that sometimes the greatest revolution starts not with a shout, but with a poem whispered on a Memphis porch at twilight.

62

What Value?

In a world increasingly focused on metrics and measurements, these stories remind us that a life's true worth can never be calculated in dollars and cents. From Miss Geneva's letter-writing ministry in Abbeville to Sister Margaret's healing gardens in Charleston, we've witnessed how single individuals can transform their corners of the South through simple acts of devotion.

The Bicycle Angel of Itta Bena doesn't measure her success in profit margins but in the wobbling first rides of children discovering freedom on two wheels. The story keeper of Beaufort doesn't count her wealth in bank statements but in preserved voices that might otherwise have been lost to time. The Letter Lady's richest moments come not from monetary transactions, but from helping hearts connect across distances.

Each of these everyday saints teaches us that life's most precious currencies aren't found in vaults:

- The patience of Brother James as he pedals mountain

roads to reach isolated souls

- The gentle wisdom of Miss Ruby Mae nurturing broken dreams in Nashville
- The loving hands of Miss Pearlie Mae preserving community memories in Monroeville
- The quiet dedication of Uncle Bill teaching troubled youth to create beauty from raw wood

They show us that value isn't something you calculate—it's something you create through:
- The courage to see possibility in broken things
- The patience to nurture growth in barren places
- The wisdom to understand that every life has purpose
- The faith to believe that small actions can yield mighty harvests

These Southern inspirations remind us that our worth isn't measured by
- The size of our bank accounts
- The grandeur of our homes
- The titles after our names
- The cars in our driveways

Instead, it's measured by
- The lives we touch
- The hope we nurture
- The love we share

- The legacy we leave in hearts rather than ledgers

Perhaps that's the deepest lesson these stories teach us—that a life's true value lies not in what we accumulate, but in what we give away. Each of our featured souls has found their worth by pouring themselves out in service to others, by seeing value in the overlooked, and by believing that every life matters, every story counts, and every soul has purpose.

In the end, we can't put a price on
- A child's first successful bike ride
- A lost soul finding their way home
- A broken spirit learning to hope again
- A forgotten story preserved for future generations

These are the real treasures of the South—not our ante-bellum mansions or our historic landmarks, but our every-day saints who prove that love is still the greatest currency of all, that service is the truest measure of wealth, and that a life lived for others is beyond any earthly value we could calculate.

For in these lives of quiet dedication, we find our truest inspiration and our greatest hope—that each of us, in our own way, can become part of this precious legacy of love that enriches our Southern soil and nurtures future generations with the timeless truth that every life has infinite worth when lived in service to others.

63

In Closing

Sacred Illuminations

In gathering these stories of Southern light, we've done more than chronicle the way sunshine plays across cotton fields or how moonlight silvers Spanish moss. We've traced the luminous threads that bind our region's soul together—each story a testament to how light reveals not just what we see, but who we are.

From the last gas lamps of Charleston to the midnight glow of Jekyll Club, from tobacco barn sunbeams to fire tower vigils, we've witnessed how light transforms the ordinary into the sacred. These aren't just tales of illumination—they're parables of persistence, of beauty that survives change, of hope that glows steadfast in the darkness.

The phosphorescent waves off our coast remind us that even in darkness, light finds a way to dance. The ancient glass in Savannah's windows teaches us that imperfection can create its own kind of beauty. The light in Miss Sarah Beth's eyes shows us how inner luminescence can outlast any shadow that life casts.

These collected moments of light tell a larger story—of a South that holds fast to its grace while embracing change, of people who understand that some things are worth preserving not because they're efficient, but because they're beautiful. In the glow of Bellingrath's garden nights, in the flash of lightning over Providence Canyon, in the steady beam of coastal lighthouses, we read our own story of endurance and transformation.

Light, in all its Southern manifestations, becomes our teacher. It shows us how to hold both past and future in the same gentle glow, how to find beauty in decay, how to keep faith with what matters. From dawn's first touch on the Chattahoochee to the last evening ray through cathedral live oaks, light reminds us that every moment carries its own particular grace.

Perhaps that's the deepest truth these stories share—that light isn't just something we see, but something we carry within. Like the fire tower watchers in their glass houses in the sky, like the lamplighters of Charleston tending their eternal flames, like the lighthouse women keeping their coastal vigils, we are all keepers of light in our own way.

As these tales return to the darkness from which they came, may they leave behind their own kind of luminescence. May they remind us that in the South, light has always been more than mere illumination—it's been our witness, our companion, our guide through changing times. In its glow, we find our way forward while keeping faith with all that came before.

And so, we close this collection with a blessing: May your path be lit by gentle Southern light. May you find grace in its glow, strength in its persistence, and hope in its eternal return. For in the end, these stories of light are really stories of us all—of how we endure, how we transform, how we keep burning bright against the darkness, one precious moment of illumination at a time.

Other Books by Dr. Charles E. Cravey at:

Https://drcharlescravey.com or

Amazon.com, Books-a-Million.com